Nelson English

Developing Fiction Skills

4

BOOK FOUR

John Jackman   Wendy Wren

OXFORD
UNIVERSITY PRESS

Contents

The Silver Sword

The Silver Sword by Ian Serraillier, is a fictional story that is based on real events which took place in Poland during the Second World War (1939–45). In the story, Ruth and Edek are left to fend for themselves and their young sister, Bronia, after their parents are taken away by German soldiers.

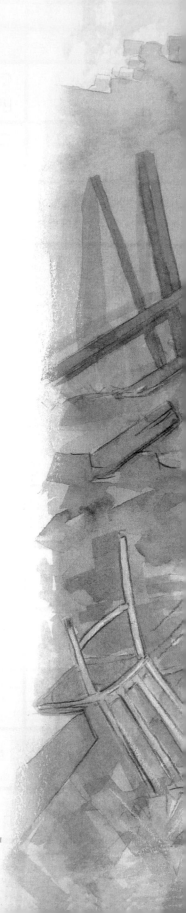

They made their new home in a cellar at the other end of the city. They had tunnelled their way into it. From the street it looked like a rabbit's burrow in a mound of rubble, with part of a wall rising behind. On the far side there was a hole in the lower part of the wall, and this let in light and air as well as rain.

When they asked the Polish Council of Protection about their mother, they were told she had been taken off to Germany to work on the land. Nobody could say which part of Germany. Though they went many times to ask, they never found out any more. 'The war will end soon,' they were told. 'Be patient, and your mother will come back.'

But the war dragged on, and their patience was to be sorely tried.

They quickly made their new home as comfortable as they could. Edek, who could climb like a monkey, scaled three storeys of a bombed building to fetch a mattress and some curtains. The mattress he gave to Ruth and Bronia. The curtains made good sheets. On wet days they could be used over the hole in the wall to keep the rain out. With floorboards he made two beds, chairs and a table. With bricks from the rubble he built a wall to divide the cellar into two rooms, one to live in and one to sleep in. He stole blankets from a Nazi supply dump, one for each of them.

Here they lived for the rest of that winter and the following spring.

Food was not easy to find. Ruth and Bronia had green Polish ration cards and were allowed to draw the small

rations that the Nazis allowed. But, except when Edek
found casual work, they had no money to buy food. Edek had
no ration card. He had not dared to apply for one, as that
would have meant disclosing his age. Everyone over twelve
had to register, and he would almost certainly have been
carried off to Germany as a slave worker. Whenever possible
they ate at the soup kitchens which Polish Welfare had set
up. Sometimes they begged at a nearby convent. Sometimes
they stole from the Nazis or scrounged from their garbage
bins. They saw nothing wrong in stealing from their enemies,
but they were careful never to steal from their own people.

Comprehension

A 1 Where did the children make their new home?

2 What had happened to their mother?

3 How did the children use the following items?

    a curtains   **b** floorboards   **c** bricks

4 How did Edek get the blankets?

5 Why did Edek have no ration card?

B 1 **a** In the extract, what is the cellar compared to?

    b In the extract, what is Edek's ability to climb compared to?

2 Write each of the following words and phrases in your own words.

    a their patience was to be sorely tried   **b** scaled

    c casual work   **d** disclosing his age

3 Think carefully about the situation in which the children find themselves. Write a list of words and phrases to describe how you think they felt during their time living in the cellar.

C 1 Is the extract in the first person or the third person?

2 Find the fourth paragraph, which begins: 'They quickly made their new home as comfortable as they could.' Imagine you are Edek. Rewrite the fourth paragraph in the first person.

 Vocabulary

Homophones and homonyms

Remember, **homophones** are words that sound the same, but are spelled differently, and **homonyms** are words that sound and are spelled the same, but have different meanings. For example:

Homophones: After the bombing, he was in a <u>daze</u> for several <u>days</u>.

Homonyms: They bought the bed in the <u>spring</u> but, by summer, a <u>spring</u> had broken.

A 1 Look again at the passage on pages 4–5. It contains many homophones. Find and write down the word from the passage that is a homophone of each word below.

    a whole   **b** heir   **c** reign   **d** there

    e bean   **f** moor   **g** knew   **h** stories

2 Copy any other words in the passage that have homophones.

B These homonyms are from the passage:

> light   back   rest   draw

Write two short sentences using each one, to show that it can have different meanings.

If necessary, use a dictionary to help you.

Spelling

Roots, prefixes and suffixes

Remember, **roots** are words or parts of words to which **prefixes** and **suffixes** can be added to make words from the same word family.
Roots, prefixes and suffixes can help with your spelling. Common ones become familiar, and help you to break up a word into sections.
They often provide a clue about the meaning as well. For example:

The Silver Sword <u>**describes**</u> events which really happened.

The root, 'scribere', comes from Latin and means 'to write'. 'Scribe', 'scribble', 'manuscript' and 'inscription' share the same root.

A Write down the root from the box that goes with each pair of words below.

Key:

L = Latin   G = Greek

mille (L) thousand	*audire* (L) to hear
capere (L) to take hold	*hydor* (G) water
navis (L) ship	*aster* (G) star
spiro (L) breathe	*prima* (L) first

Some words have more than one root. For example:
<u>autograph</u>

1	perspire	respiration	2	audible	audience
5	asterisk	astrology	4	hydrant	hydraulic
5	millennium	millipede	6	primary	premier
7	captive	capable	8	navigation	navy

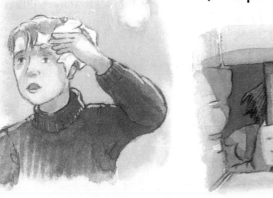

B Copy each word below and underline its root. Use a dictionary to check the meanings of the words in each group, then write down what you think each root means.

1 photograph   telephoto   photosynthesis
2 telescope   microscope   bioscope
3 atmosphere   spherical   bathysphere
4 export   import   portable

Grammar

Word classes

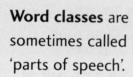

Word classes are sometimes called 'parts of speech'.

There are the eight main **word classes**, or types, depending on the work the word does in a sentence.

Class	Description	Examples
noun	a naming word	telephone London
pronoun	takes the place of a noun	they he it me
adjective	describes a noun or pronoun	green small
verb	an action or doing word	came spoke jump
	a being word	was be am
adverb	describes the action of a verb or adds to an adjective	slowly tomorrow
conjunction	a joining word	and but until
interjection	an exclamation	oh! ouch!
preposition	shows the relationship between two things or people	on for in

A 1 Copy the coloured words from the sentences below. Next to each word, state what class of word it is in that sentence.

   a "Ouch! I scratched **myself** on **that** rusty **nail**," said Edek.

   b They made **their** new **home** in a cellar.

   c The children quickly **made** their new home as comfortable **as** they could.

   d The parents of Bronia, **Edek** and Ruth are taken **away** by soldiers.

2 Read the passage on pages 4–5 again. Find and write down:

   a four common nouns   **b** four proper nouns

   c four verbs   **d** four adjectives

   e four pronouns   **f** four prepositions

Remember, words that are spelled the same but have different meanings are called **homonyms**.

Some words can be used in more than one way, and so can be used as more than one class of word. For example:

    I wish I could <u>fly</u> away.   There was a <u>fly</u> on the cellar wall.

              verb   noun

B 1 Write the words from the box that can be used as both a noun and a verb.

> build   tie   fire   rule   Poland   brush   lift   cellar

2 Choose three pairs of homonyms from question 1 and use each pair in a single sentence of your own.

Punctuation

Capital letters and punctuation

Capital letters and **punctuation marks** are important in helping the reader understand what you have written. For example:

> they made their new home in a cellar at the other end of the city they had tunnelled their way into it from the street it looked like a rabbits burrow in a mound of rubble with part of a wall rising behind

Now, look back to the beginning of the extract on page 4 to see how much easier the above passage is to read when the capital letters and punctuation are in place.

Remember, **proper nouns** need capital letters.

A In these sentences, the punctuation and capital letters have been omitted. Copy each sentence, writing it correctly.

1 bronia edek and ruth missed their parents terribly

2 they were living in poland having escaped from the german soldiers

3 eventually after looking for some time they found a cellar

4 edek who could climb like a monkey scaled three storeys of a bombed building

5 i wouldnt like to live in a cellar would you

B The following passage from *The Silver Sword* is about the children escaping at night in two canoes. It is difficult to read without punctuation. Copy it, adding capital letters and punctuation.

the current was swift in the darkness the great wooded hills swept by for a moment the moon peeped from a cloud and turned the rippling surface to silver side by side the two canoes sped on along the left bank the line of hills curved downwards were those dim shapes houses had they reached the village again the moon appeared it had chosen quite the wrong moment for this was indeed the village with houses crowded about both banks and on the left bank suddenly an open space with lorries in it they were so close together they were almost touching and there were several rows of them these must be the lorries that were to take the polish refugees back to poland with a tightening of fear in her throat ruth realised that if they were spotted now they would be taken back too

Writing

The story teller

Most stories are told from the **point of view** of:
- a person who was involved – a first-person account
- a person who was not involved – a third-person account.

The Silver Sword is a third-person account, as the narrator (the person 'telling' the story) is not a character in the story.

Sometimes, a story is made up of several first-hand accounts by different people who were involved. This helps the reader to see different points of view, and to be told things by each narrator that other characters might not have known.

A In Comprehension part C (page 6), you rewrote the fourth paragraph in the first person, from Edek's point of view. Rewrite it again as if you were Ruth.

B You are going to plan and write about an event which happens to the children. Think about:
- what might happen to them
- whether to introduce other characters
- whether the incident happened in the cellar or in a new setting.

Write about the event twice:

1 as Ruth would have related it
2 as Edek would have related it.

You will need to write in the first person. The passage doesn't tell us much about Ruth and Edek, so you will have to imagine how their characters might be different. You need to make sure your two accounts are not too similar. Think about:
- the different ways in which Ruth and Edek might react
- whether the children were together the whole time
- whether their feelings during the event were different.

Robinson Crusoe

Robinson Crusoe, written by Daniel Defoe, was first published in 1719. It is the story of a young man who runs away to sea and is shipwrecked. This extract tells of how he survived the shipwreck and landed on a South Sea island. As the story was written nearly 300 years ago, the language and style may seem a little unusual.

Nothing can describe the confusion of thought which I felt when I sunk into the water; for though I swam very well, yet I could not deliver myself from the waves so as to draw breath, till that wave having driven me, or rather carried me, a vast way on towards the shore and, having spent itself, went back, and left me upon the land almost dry, but half dead with the water I took in. I had so much presence of mind as well as breath left, that seeing myself nearer the mainland than expected, I got upon my feet, and endeavoured to make on towards the land as fast as I could, before another wave should return and take me up again. But I soon found it was impossible to avoid it ...

The wave that came upon me again, buried me at once twenty or thirty feet deep in its own body, and I could feel myself carried with a mighty force and swiftness towards the shore a very great way. But I held my breath and assisted myself to swim still forward with all my might. I was ready to burst with holding my breath, when, as I felt myself rising up, so, to my immediate relief, I found my head and hands shoot out above the surface of the water and, though it was not two seconds of time I could keep myself so, yet it relieved me greatly, gave me breath and new courage. I was covered again with water a good while, but not so long but I held it out; and finding the water had spent itself and began to return, I struck forward against the return of the waves, and felt ground again with my feet. I stood still a few moments to recover my breath, and till the water went from me, and then took to my heels, and run with what strength I had farther towards the shore. But neither would this deliver me from the fury of the sea, which came pouring in after me again, and twice more I was lifted up by the waves, and carried forwards as before, the shore being very flat.

The last of these two had well near been fatal to me, for the sea, having hurried me along as before, landed me, or rather dashed me, against a piece of rock, and that with such force as it left me senseless, and indeed helpless, as to my own deliverance. For the blow, taking my side and breast, beat the breath as it were quite out of my body and, had it returned again immediately, I must have been strangled in the water but I recovered a little before the return of the waves, and seeing I should be covered again with the water, I resolved to hold fast by a piece of rock, and so to hold my breath, if possible, till the wave went back. Now as the waves were not so high as at first, being nearer land, I held my hold till the wave abated, and then fetched another run, which brought me so near the shore that the next wave, though it went over me, yet did not so swallow me up as to carry me away, and the next run I took, I got to the mainland, where, to my great comfort, I clambered up the cliffs of the shore and sat me down upon the grass, free from danger, and quite out of reach of the water.

 ## Comprehension

A Write whether each sentence is true or false.

1 The shipwrecked man could not swim.
2 He did not swallow any water.
3 The waves threw him against a rock.
4 He clutched a rock to avoid being carried out to sea.
5 The waves nearer the shore were bigger than those farther out.
6 He did not make it to land.

B 1 Write down a word or phrase from the passage which means the same as each of the following words or phrases.

a long distance   b tried
c great speed   d come back

2 Explain in your own words each of the following phrases.

a presence of mind   b with all my might
c took to my heels   d well near been fatal to me

C 1 Who is telling the story?
2 Write a summary in the third person of what happened to Robinson Crusoe in the passage.

Australia

Vocabulary

Our changing language

Some of the old-fashioned language in *Robinson Crusoe* sounds a little strange today. For example:

> … though I swam well, I could not deliver myself from the waves so as to draw breath …

Just as the way we express ourselves changes, words and their spellings also **change** gradually over time. For example, today we say 'book' but, 300 years ago, it was spelled 'booke'. Today we say 'certain' but, 300 years ago, it was spelled 'sarten'.

A **1** Write the modern version of each of these words.

a	shouldst	b	yonder	c	gavest	d	kin
e	shalt	f	hath	g	saith	h	wilt
i	thou	j	cometh	k	spake	l	art

2 Write each of these sentences in more modern language. Use a dictionary to help you find the meaning of any words you cannot guess.

a Come hither and take thine ease awhile.

b Ist mine adversary nigh?

c Be not afraid, I pray you.

d Thou wouldst fain take thy leave, I'll warrant.

B Write these phrases, written by Daniel Defoe, in the style he might have used had he been writing today.

1 I got upon my feet and endeavoured to make on towards the land

2 I could not deliver myself from the waves

3 though it was not two seconds of time

4 yet it relieved me greatly

5 I resolved to hold fast by a piece of rock

Spelling

Prefixes

Having a knowledge of **prefixes** can help with your spelling, and can provide a clue about word meanings. For example:

I soon found it was <u>im</u>possible to avoid it …

The prefix 'im' usually means 'not'. 'Impossible' means 'not possible'.

A **1** Use the information in the table to help you write the meaning of each of the words below.

Prefix	Meaning
a	on
anti	opposite, against
con	together
de	down, away
fore	front, in front, beforehand
inter	between
pre	before
re	again
sub	under

a forewarn   b renew   c antibiotic

d congregate e aboard   f submerge

g descend   h interval i precaution

2 Write another word with the same prefix as each of the words in question 1.

B Copy the words below. Underline the prefix of each word. Use a dictionary to find the meanings of the words, then write what you think each prefix means.

1 *antecedent*   *anteroom*   *antenatal*

2 *aeroplane*   *aerobiology* *aerosol*

3 *microscope*   *microchip*   *microfilm*

4 *exit*   *exclaim*   *exclude*

Grammar

Active sentences

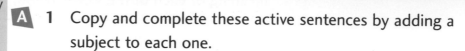
In an **active sentence**, the **subject** is the person or thing that is doing something, and the **object** is the person or thing that is having something done to it. For example:

Robinson Crusoe <u>sat</u> on the <u>shore</u>.

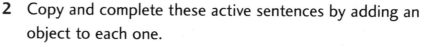

subject	verb	object

The subject and object of a sentence are usually **nouns** but can also be **pronouns**.

A 1 Copy and complete these active sentences by adding a subject to each one.

    a <u>The Ship</u> was wrecked during the storm.

    b <u>Robinson Crusoe</u> nearly drowned in the rough sea.

    c <u>The wave</u> forced him twenty or thirty feet under the surface.

    d <u>Robinson Crusoe</u> struggled to reach the shore.

2 Copy and complete these active sentences by adding an object to each one.

    a Robinson Crusoe clung desperately to <u>dry land</u>

    b Eventually, he reached <u>the Island</u>

    c He sat down on <u>the grass</u> to recover.

    d He realised he was stranded alone, on <u>the Island</u>.

B Use these subjects and objects in active sentences of your own.

	subject	object
1	fish	food
2	ship	sea
3	rope	hammock
4	wood	hut

Sentence construction

Connectives and conjunctions

Words and phrases that connect other phrases and clauses in a sentence are called **connectives** or **conjunctions**. For example:
I struggled ashore just in time, <u>for</u> I was exhausted.

A Copy each sentence, adding a suitable connective word or phrase. Do not use 'and', 'but' or 'then'!

1 My lungs were bursting _____ I suddenly broke the surface of the water.

2 I had received a blow on my head _____ I clung to the rock for support.

3 My head told me I should find shelter _____ my body told me I needed a rest.

4 It was getting dark _____ I decided to try to make a fire.

5 You might imagine my reaction _____ I saw footprints in the sand.

B Look at the passage on pages 12–13. Find and copy two sentences that contain a connective or a conjunction. Underline the connective or conjunction in each.

Writing

First person

Daniel Defoe wrote the story of *Robinson Crusoe* in the **first person**, as if he was Robinson Crusoe and the adventure had happened to him. Robinson Crusoe tells us:

- what happened, for example:
  'I could feel myself carried with a mighty force'
- what he felt like, for example:
  'I was ready to burst with holding my breath'.

You should write in the first person when:

- you are writing about something that actually happened to you – autobiography
- you are writing about something that you imagine has happened to you or the character you are writing as – fiction written in an autobiographical style.

When you are writing in the first person, you should avoid starting every sentence with 'I', which can become boring. For example:

I went down to the sea early that morning. I looked at the ships.
I noticed one of them was leaning to the side. I watched as it sank lower and lower into the water. I saw it slip under the waves.

The piece of writing can be improved by changing the order of the words. For example:

Early that morning I went down to the sea. I looked at the ships.
I noticed one of them was leaning to the side. As I watched, it sank lower and lower into the water. I saw it slip under the waves.

We can improve the above passage even more by using conjunctions. For example:

Early that morning I went down to the sea. I looked at the ships and noticed that one of them was leaning to the side. As I watched, it sank lower and lower into the water until it slipped under the waves.

A 1 Improve this text by changing the order of the words.

I like to watch the waves when I go to the seaside. I enjoy swimming although I'm not very good at it. I always feel tired when I have had a swim!

2 Improve this passage by using conjunctions to join the sentences together.

I saw a spider in the bath. I ran out of the room. I called my mother. I asked her to catch it. I said that she should throw the spider out of the window.

3 Rewrite the following passage, improving it by changing the order of the words and joining some sentences together.

I went swimming yesterday. I had been given goggles for my birthday. I wanted to try them out. I knew that the swimming pool opened at ten o'clock. I caught the half-past seven bus. I was the first one there. I had the pool to myself for half an hour. I had a lovely swim. I really enjoyed myself.

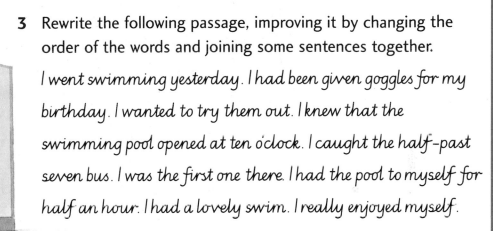

B Imagine you are in the same situation as Robinson Crusoe, washed up on the shore of a desert island. What is the island like? What do you do? Remember:

- write in the first person
- describe what you see
- describe what you do
- describe how you feel
- think of interesting ways to begin your sentences – don't start every one with 'I'.

Hard Times

Charles Dickens was a very famous Victorian writer. Here is a passage from his book, *Hard Times*, in which Mr Thomas Gradgrind is teaching a class. Mr Gradgrind is not interested in what the children think or feel, he is only interested in facts!

"Girl number twenty," said Mr Gradgrind, squarely pointing with his square forefinger, "I don't know that girl. Who is that girl?"

"Sissy Jupe, sir," explained number twenty, blushing, standing up, and curtseying.

"Sissy is not a name," said Mr Gradgrind. "Don't call yourself Sissy. Call yourself Cecilia."

"It's father as calls me Sissy, sir," returned the young girl in a trembling voice, and with another curtsey.

"Then he has no business to do it," said Mr Gradgrind. "Tell him he mustn't. Cecilia Jupe. Let me see. What is your father?"

"He belongs to the horse-riding, if you please, sir."

Mr Gradgrind frowned, and waved off the objectionable calling with his hand.

"We don't want to know anything about that, here. You mustn't tell us about that, here. Your father breaks horses, don't he?"

"If you please, sir, when they can get any to break, they do break horses in the ring, sir ..."

"Very well, then ... Give me your definition of a horse."

(Sissy Jupe thrown into the greatest alarm by this demand.)

"Girl number twenty unable to define a horse!" said Mr Gradgrind ... "Girl number twenty possessed of no facts, in reference to one of the commonest of animals! Some boy's definition of a horse. Bitzer, yours ..."

"Quadruped. Graminivorous. Forty teeth, namely twenty-four grinders, four eye-teeth, and twelve incisors. Sheds coat in the spring; in marshy countries, sheds hoofs too. Hoofs hard, but requiring to be shod with iron. Age known by marks in mouth."

"Now girl number twenty," said Mr Gradgrind. "You know what a horse is."

GLOSSARY
breaks horses trains horses
calling job or profession
graminivorous grass-eating
quadruped four-footed animal

 Comprehension

A
1 Who is girl number twenty?
2 What does her father do?
3 How does she react when she is asked to define a horse?
4 Who gives a definition of a horse that Mr Gradgrind approves of?

B
1 Would you like Mr Gradgrind as a teacher? Give your reasons.
2 What does the fact that Sissy was known as 'girl number twenty' tell you about the kind of school it was?
3 Do you think Bitzer's description of a horse is a good one?
4 Define a horse in your own words.
5 Do you think that Mr Gradgrind is right about only wanting to know facts?

C Imagine you are going to turn this story extract into a playscript. Carefully read the extract again, and look at the illustration.
1 Write a few sentences to describe the setting of the play.
2 Make a list of the people who would be in the play. Write the names of the characters who would have speaking parts.
3 Draw a sketch of how the stage would be set, showing the scenery and props you would use.

Vocabulary

Origins of words

The names of the months come from Latin – the language spoken by the Romans, who lived 2,000 years ago. The word 'September' comes from the Latin word *septem*, meaning 'seven', but September is the ninth month! The reason is that, in Roman times, September was the seventh month, but Roman leaders Julius Caesar and Augustus Caesar both wanted a month named after them, so two more months were added.

Remember, the months were named when there were only 10 in the Roman year, before two extra ones were added.

A Match the name of each month with its Roman origin. Write the twelve months and their origins in the correct order.

March	based on *Septem*, the Latin word for 'seven'
August	named after Mars, the Roman god of war
April	named after Maia, a Roman goddess
November	named after Augustus Caesar
February	named after Juno, queen of the Roman gods
September	named after Janus, the Roman god who protects doorways
July	based on Februa, the Roman feast of purification
May	based on the Latin word for 'nine'
October	named after Julius Caesar
December	based on the Latin word for 'eight'
January	based on the Latin word for 'ten'
June	based on *aperire*, the Latin word for 'to open'

In Roman times, the days of the week were named after the Sun, the Moon and the five planets that the Romans knew about – Saturn, Mars, Mercury, Jupiter and Venus.

B 1 Write the three days of the week that still have names based on their original Roman names.

The other four days of the week are said to be named after other gods and goddesses from long ago – Thor, Woden, Tiw and Freya.

2 Write down which day of the week is named after each of these gods and goddesses.

Spelling

Difficult words

A Below are 30 words people often have difficulty spelling. Use your memory to copy and complete them correctly.

1 jew_l
2 mini_ture
3 sep_rate
4 cus_ion
5 libra_y
6 shep_erd
7 parli_ment
8 con_ _ious
9 cu_board
10 enco_rage
11 happ_ness
12 burgl_r
13 ex_ell_nt
14 justi_e
15 reco_ni_e
16 nei_ _bour
17 vill_ _n
18 rec_ _ve
19 beca_se
20 admi_ _ion
21 addi_ _on
22 grud_e
23 presen_e
24 miser_ble
25 photogra_ _
26 c_oir
27 colum_
28 obstin_te
29 a_kward
30 obst_cle

B Now use your dictionary to check your spelling of each word. Make a separate list of those you found difficult, and try to learn them using the 'look, cover, say, write, check' method.

Grammar

Simple and compound sentences

A **simple sentence** is made up of one main clause. For example:
   Mr Thomas Gradgrind is a teacher.

A **compound sentence** is made up of two or more simple sentences joined by a **conjunction**. For example:

Simple sentence:	Mr Thomas Gradgrind is a teacher.
Simple sentence:	He is only interested in facts.
Compound sentence:	Mr Thomas Gradgrind is a teacher, and he is only interested in facts.

| clause | clause | conjunction |

Simple sentence:	A new girl has started at his school.
Simple sentence:	She has not learnt many facts.
Compound sentence:	A new girl has started at his school, but she has not learned many facts.

| clause | clause | conjunction |

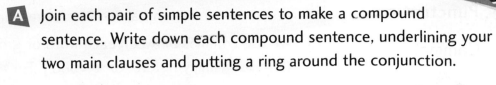

A Join each pair of simple sentences to make a compound sentence. Write down each compound sentence, underlining your two main clauses and putting a ring around the conjunction.

1 A new girl is starting school today.

   I hope she will sit next to me.

2 Her name is Catherine.

   She likes to be called Cathy.

3 Cathy says she is glad she is coming to our school.

   She has heard that our teacher is very kind.

4 I hope Cathy and I will be friends.

   I will still be friends with Rosie.

5 I will take Cathy to the classroom.

   She does not know her way around school yet.

B Add a conjunction and another main clause to make each of these simple sentences into a compound sentence.

1 Cathy's family is from Leeds _____

2 Cathy and I ate our lunch together _____

3 She was nervous on her first day at school _____

   _____

4 Our teacher showed Cathy where to hang her coat _____

   _____

Punctuation

Commas

Remember, we use **commas** for various reasons:

1 We use commas between each word or group of words in a list (but not usually before 'or' or 'and'). For example:

In Victorian times there were no cars, computers, televisions, videos or aeroplanes.

Today we have computers, CDs, personal stereos and mobile phones.

2 We use commas between the parts of a sentence (phrases and clauses), where the reader needs to make a short pause. For example:

The idea of sending postcards, which came from Austria, became very popular in Victorian times.

Life was hard for poorer people in Victorian times, wasn't it?

3 In direct speech, we use commas to separate the actual words spoken from the rest of the sentence. If the speech comes first, the comma goes inside the quotation marks. If the speaker's name comes first, the comma goes after that phrase. For example:

"Open your books," ordered Mr Gradgrind.

Sissy mumbled, "I do not have any books, sir."

A Copy these sentences, adding the missing commas.

1 Plates of sandwiches bowls of salad slices of cold meat loaves of bread jugs of milk pots of tea and a huge cake were spread out on the table.

2 The white-faced girl with a cry of alarm ran up the stairs.

3 Dickens's books such as Hard Times and Oliver Twist give us a view of how some children especially the poorer ones suffered in nineteenth-century Britain.

B Copy this passage of dialogue, adding the missing commas.

"I'm pleased that I live now and not 100 years ago" said Mark.

"So am I" replied his sister "as Victorian teachers seemed very strict."

"I wonder" mused Mark "whether Mrs Lindsay would be so harsh with us?"

"Oh no" cried Lucy. "I'm sure she wouldn't."

Writing

Playscripts

Just like a story, a **playscript** needs:
- plot
- setting
- characters.

But you must remember that the audience will be watching the play being acted, not reading it.

The actors and actresses read the **script** to find out what they have to say. Remember, the **stage directions** tell them how to say some of the lines and what movements they must make.

A 1 Sissy, Bitzer and Mr Gradgrind are the main characters in the passage from *Hard Times* on pages 20–21. Make notes on each of these characters to show what kind of people you think they are.

2 There were many other children in the classroom. If the passage was written as a playscript, they would be called 'non-speaking parts' because they do not say anything. Make notes on how they might behave to show their reactions when:
- Mr Gradgrind is talking to Sissy
- he gets cross when she cannot define a horse
- he looks around for a boy to define a horse.

The children would probably react in different ways.

B Write the extract from *Hard Times* as a playscript. Look back at your answer to part C of the Comprehension work on page 22 to help you. Remember to include:
- a list of the characters and who they are
- the setting
- the dialogue, showing who says what
- stage directions.

You can add stage directions for the non-speaking parts as a group, by calling them 'The pupils' or by giving a few of them names and writing individual stage directions.

The Listeners

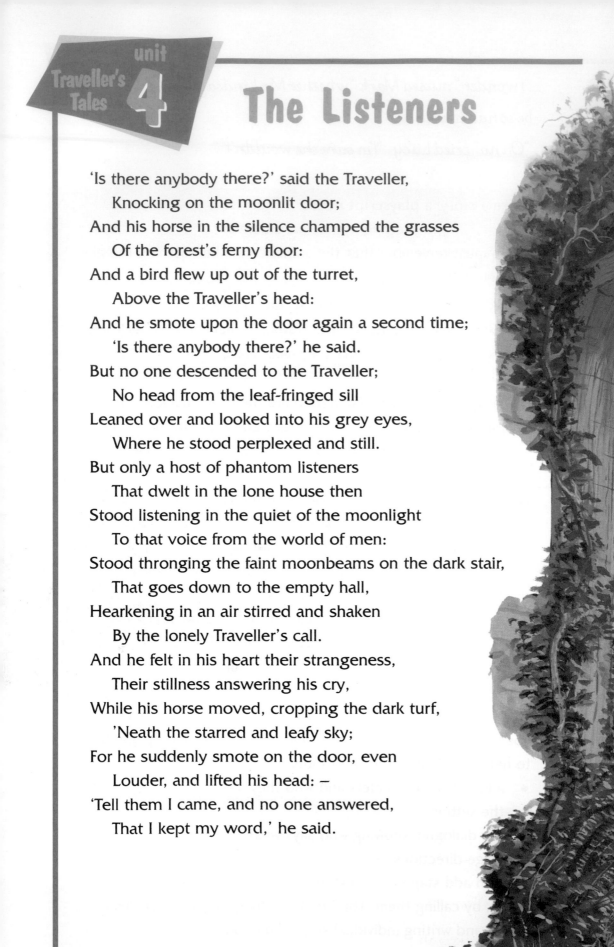

'Is there anybody there?' said the Traveller,
    Knocking on the moonlit door;
And his horse in the silence champed the grasses
    Of the forest's ferny floor:
And a bird flew up out of the turret,
    Above the Traveller's head:
And he smote upon the door again a second time;
    'Is there anybody there?' he said.
But no one descended to the Traveller;
    No head from the leaf-fringed sill
Leaned over and looked into his grey eyes,
    Where he stood perplexed and still.
But only a host of phantom listeners
    That dwelt in the lone house then
Stood listening in the quiet of the moonlight
    To that voice from the world of men:
Stood thronging the faint moonbeams on the dark stair,
    That goes down to the empty hall,
Hearkening in an air stirred and shaken
    By the lonely Traveller's call.
And he felt in his heart their strangeness,
    Their stillness answering his cry,
While his horse moved, cropping the dark turf,
    'Neath the starred and leafy sky;
For he suddenly smote on the door, even
    Louder, and lifted his head: –
'Tell them I came, and no one answered,
    That I kept my word,' he said.

Never the least stir made the listeners,
    Though every word he spake
Fell echoing through the shadowiness of the still house
    From the one man left awake:
Ay, they heard his foot upon the stirrup,
    And the sound of iron on stone,
And how the silence surged softly backward,
When the plunging hoofs were gone.

by Walter de la Mare

 Comprehension **A** 1 Does the action of the poem take place during the day or at night?

2 Is the setting of the poem in a town or in the country?

3 How had the Traveller travelled?

4 What colour were the Traveller's eyes?

B This is a very mysterious poem and there are lots of things it doesn't tell us. Use your imagination to answer these questions.

1 Who is 'the Traveller'?

2 Why has he gone to the house?

3 Who is he expecting to meet there?

4 Who are the 'phantom listeners'?

5 Why is there no one there to meet him?

6 What is the promise he made?

7 Why is he described as 'the one man left awake'?

C Now you have thought about what might be happening in the poem, write two paragraphs:

- paragraph 1: a summary of what you think the poem is about
- paragraph 2: how the poem makes you feel, whether you like the poem or not and why.

Vocabulary

Our changing language

You have learned how our language has **changed** over time. In some ways, English is now changing faster than ever with new words being needed to name new technologies, new fashions, new games, etc. For example:

> space shuttle   aeroplanes   internet   cars

A Look at this picture. Write the names of as many things as possible that a person living 100 years ago would not have known.

B Imagine you are writing a dictionary of modern words for somebody who lived 100 years ago. Write a definition of each of the following words or phrases.

1 monorail	2 bungee jump	3 snowboard
4 theme park	5 helicopter	6 burger bar

Spelling

Unstressed vowels

Unstressed vowels are vowels which we either do not sound, or do not sound very distinctly, as we speak. Unstressed vowels can cause spelling problems because it is easy to forget them and miss them out.

For example:

list<u>e</u>ner

'List<u>e</u>ner' sounds like 'listner' because the 'e' is an unstressed vowel.

A Copy these words. Circle the unstressed vowels.

1 chocolate   2 difference   3 valuable

4 traveller   5 usually   6 desperate

7 factory   8 business   9 victory

B Write the correct spellings of these words, putting in the unstressed vowels.

1 vegtables   2 evry   3 intresting

4 temprature   5 dictionry   6 boundry

Grammar

Active and passive

Remember, every sentence needs a verb. If the action of the verb is done by the subject of the sentence, we call it an **active verb**, and it is an **active sentence**. For example:

<u>The horse</u> <u>champed</u> the grass.

subject	verb

If the subject of the sentence has the action of the verb done to it, we call it a **passive verb**, and it is a **passive sentence**. For example:

<u>The grass</u> <u>was champed</u> by the horse.

subject	verb

Passive verbs need an auxiliary or 'helper' verb, such as 'were' or 'was'.

A Copy the verb in each sentence. State whether it is active or passive.

1 The traveller rode along the track.

2 His hair was ruffled by the breeze.

3 The moonlight was blocked by the tall trees.

4 The horse's hooves clattered on the stones.

B 1 Change these sentences from active to passive.

a Somebody closed and locked the door.

b The sounds of night creatures filled the forest.

c A throng of silent listeners inhabited the house.

2 Change these sentences from passive to active.

a The sky was lit by millions of stars.

b The traveller's horse was startled by a fox's cry.

c The traveller was watched by an owl perched in a tree.

Punctuation

Colons and semi-colons

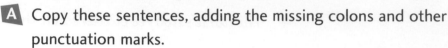

Colons are sometimes used at the beginning of a list or a quotation. For example:

For the school trip, you will need to bring: a packed lunch, warm clothing, wellington boots, a notebook and a pen.

The opening line of my favourite poem is: 'I love chocolate cake'.

A Copy these sentences, adding the missing colons and other punctuation marks.

1 We have been asked to choose a poem by one of the following poets Lewis Carroll Charles Causley T S Eliot Edward Lear Michael Rosen and Wes Magee

2 These are my favourite poems by Roger McGough First Day at School The Sound Collector Valentine Poem and The Fight of the Year

3 Our instructions for homework were choose a poem copy it draw a picture to go with it and practise reading it aloud

Semi-colons are used between the clauses in a compound sentence instead of a conjunction. For example:

Miss Ross loves poetry; she reads us some brilliant poems!

B Copy these sentences, adding the missing semi-colons and other punctuation marks.

1 Our teachers lessons are always interesting and fun we were all very unhappy when we heard she will be leaving the school

2 She studied art at college she wants to teach pottery

3 We begin our lessons listening to our teacher we end lessons discussing what we have learned

Writing

Poetry

A good **poem** makes readers react in some way. It may make them feel sad, frightened, amused, puzzled.

When you read 'The Listeners' you probably felt puzzled because there were so many unanswered questions, and possibly you felt sorry for the Traveller.

When you write your own poems, you must think carefully about how you want readers to react.

A Write a poem about a traveller. You can use one of these suggestions or you can use your own idea.

The traveller likes to wander from place to place. Your readers will think what a wonderful life the traveller has, being free to roam around.

The traveller has to deliver an urgent message, and the journey is long and hard.

Your reader will be anxious that the traveller gets to his/her destination and saves the day.

The traveller is being pursued and is moving at great speed to get away.

Your reader is frightened for the traveller and wants him/her to escape before something awful happens.

B Imagine you are one of the 'phantom listeners' in 'The Listeners'. You know the Traveller is outside, but you do not answer the door. Write your own mysterious poem. Think about:
- why you and the other listeners are in the house
- who the listeners are
- why you do not answer the door.

The Mystery of the Mary Celeste

Some stories are based on events that really happened. Writers use some of the basic facts, but may change some details and add others of their own. Below is a fictional version of a mysterious event that really happened.

On 5th December, 1872, the *Dei Gratia*, a ship sailing across the Atlantic Ocean from New York to Gibraltar, came across a two-masted square-rigger in the middle of the ocean. Her course was unsteady, going this way and that with the wind. As the *Dei Gratia* got closer, the captain could see that no one was at the helm. He signalled to the strange ship but there was no reply.

Lowering a rowing boat into the water, the captain, the second mate and two other sailors made their way over to the ship. As they got closer, the name on the stern became visible. It was the *Mary Celeste*.

The captain and the mate climbed aboard, expecting to be greeted by members of the crew, but what they found was a mystery that they could not explain, and which remains unsolved to this day.

They made a thorough search of the ship only to find that it was completely deserted. The ship itself was in excellent condition. There was plenty of food and water, and the cargo, barrels of alcohol, was intact and in place in the hold.

In the captain's cabin they found the table laid for a breakfast which had only been half-eaten and, in the galley, pots containing food hung over a dead fire. In the mate's cabin, there was a piece of paper on the desk on which was written a half-finished calculation. The only thing that appeared to be missing was the ship's chronometer.

The captain of the *Dei Gratia* suspected that there had been a mutiny but, as the lifeboat was still there, it was impossible to

see how the crew had escaped. Had they been taken off by a passing ship? Had they jumped overboard? There were, however, some sinister clues. In one cabin there was a cutlass, smeared with blood, and there were similar stains on the deck rail.

The last entry in the *Mary Celeste*'s log was dated 24th November – ten days before the *Dei Gratia* had come across her. The log indicated that she had been passing north of St Mary's Island in the Azores. If she had been abandoned soon after that, there was no way she would have drifted to this spot. The way her sails were set, she could not have reached where she was unless someone had been sailing her.

An official inquiry came up with an explanation that did not hold water. It was decided that the most likely course of events was that the crew had murdered the captain and his family, thrown their bodies overboard and then escaped on another vessel. However, there was no sign of a struggle and no valuables were taken.

There were many popular theories at the time. It was suggested that the ship had been attacked by an octopus or some such monster, which had taken the crew but left the ship completely undamaged! Others suggested that the crew had disembarked on an unknown island and left the boat to drift away, or that they had been sucked off the decks by some bizarre whirlwind. Despite the theories, the mystery of the *Mary Celeste* has never been solved.

GLOSSARY
chronometer an instrument for measuring time, used in navigation
cutlass a type of sword
log a written record of a voyage
square-rigger a type of sailing boat

Comprehension

A 1 Across which ocean was the *Dei Gratia* sailing when the *Mary Celeste* was sighted?

2 What was it about the *Mary Celeste* that attracted the attention of the crew of the *Dei Gratia*?

3 What did the captain and the mate of the *Dei Gratia* find on the *Mary Celeste* that suggested there was no reason for the crew to abandon ship?

4 List all the things they found that were out of the ordinary.

5 The captain of the *Dei Gratia* and the official inquiry concluded that there had been a mutiny. Why was this an unlikely explanation?

6 Make a list of the other explanations which were put forward.

B 1 From the evidence in the passage, at what time of day do you think the *Mary Celeste* ran into trouble?

2 What do you think the blood-stained cutlass and deck-rail suggest?

3 Explain the following words and phrases:

   a at the helm   b was intact   c the galley

   d a mutiny   e had been abandoned   f popular theories

4 What do you think might have happened to the *Mary Celeste*?

C Carefully read the account of the *Mary Celeste* again. Based on the information from the story, briefly note down two or three other possible explanations for the mystery.

 ## Vocabulary

Idioms

Remember, **idioms** are short phrases which mean something quite different from what they say. For example:

   The official inquiry's explanation <u>did not hold water</u>.

In this sentence, the idiom 'did not hold water' means that the explanation had weaknesses.

A 1 From the box, copy the correct meaning of each idiom below.

   a in the same boat   *suspect that something is not right*

   b smell a rat   *be good at growing plants*

   c have green fingers   *make friends after an argument*

   d bury the hatchet   *in a similar position*

2 Use the four idioms from part A in sentences of your own.

B Copy and complete these idioms and write a short explanation of each one.

1 To count your chickens before they are _____.

2 To put all your cards on the _____.

3 To live from hand to _____.

4 The boot is on the other _____.

5 To tear your ___ ___ out.

Spelling

Spelling by analogy

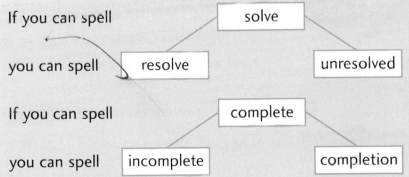

An **analogy** is a similarity. Recognising analogies between words from the same word family can help you with spelling. For example:

If you can spell   solve

you can spell   resolve   unresolved

If you can spell   complete

you can spell   incomplete   completion

A For each word below, write two more words from the same word family.

1 fear	2 compare	3 necessary
4 important	5 fortunate	6 relevant
7 memory	8 accept	9 appearance

B Look back at the passage on pages 36–37. Find six words that are members of word families. For each one, write as many other words from the family as you can.

Grammar

'is', 'are', 'was' and 'were'

The singular pronoun 'I' is an exception to the rule. The present tense is 'I <u>am</u>', the past tense is 'I <u>was</u>'.

Remember, '**is**', '**are**', '**was**' and '**were**' are 'helper' verbs that help the main verb in a sentence. They are also 'being' verbs. Here are the rules for using 'is', 'are', 'was' and 'were':

	With singular noun/pronoun	With plural noun/pronoun and 'you'
Present tense	is	are
Past tense	was	were

A 1 Copy these sentences, adding the missing verb so that each sentence is in the past tense.

a   Nobody _____ at the helm of the Mary Celeste.

b   The mate of the Dei Gratia _____ ordered by the captain to search the Mary Celeste.

c   Pots containing food _____ in the captain's cabin.

d   Food and water _____ in plentiful supply.

e   The Mary Celeste _____ in excellent condition.

Now write the sentences again in the present tense.

B Copy these sentences, correcting the mistakes.

1   The Dei Gratia's sailors was quite worried by what they saw.

2   One of them were certain a monster had taken the Mary Celeste's crew.

3   If you was there, you'd have been worried too!

4   The captain were trying to stop his men from getting too agitated.

5   What was the conclusions of the inquiry?

6   They was sure a mutiny had occurred.

Sentence construction

Avoiding repetition

Remember, **repeating** words and phrases and using words that are not needed can make your writing clumsy and less interesting.

For example:

> The reason why I think that the *Mary Celeste* caused so much distress to the crew aboard the *Dei Gratia* was because I believe that all the sailors were thoroughly scared that what happened to the *Mary Celeste* might also happen to the *Dei Gratia* and they might all disappear too.

This sentence could have been better expressed as:

> The sailors on the *Dei Gratia* were afraid that what happened to the *Mary Celeste* might happen to them.

A How short a sentence can you write that means the same as each of these long sentences?

1 The real basic cause of the actual problem of what happened to the Mary Celeste is certainly still an absolute mystery to all the people who have ever spent time thinking about what happened.

2 Over the years and as time has passed, the true facts about the Mary Celeste that are really correct have been mixed up and confused with a great deal of other things that people are saying are facts but are untrue because people have made them up or guessed so they aren't really correct.

Remember, **prepositions** are words that tell us where something is – its 'position'. For example:

> below   around   on   under

Sometimes, adding a preposition to a sentence does not add any new information. For example:

> They sat <u>down</u> in the rowing boat.

This would have made sense without the preposition 'down':

> They sat in the rowing boat.

B Copy each sentence, removing any unnecessary words.

1 The captain and the mate arrived there in a small boat.

2 They climbed up on to the deck.

3 The wind was blowing up a gale.

4 As they left, they turned around to take a last look.

Writing

Mystery stories

When writing a **mystery story**, the main aim is to keep your readers guessing and to keep some surprises until the very end. Sometimes, the mystery is not solved at all, and the readers have to use their imagination.

Mystery writers have different ways of keeping the readers' interest:

- They create **suspense** by changing the pace of the story. They might quickly gloss over less interesting parts of the story, but go into lots of detail about the mysterious parts, so that the reader is eager to find out more.
- They build up the story gradually, giving readers a few facts at a time, so that they slowly discover all the facts.
- They highlight mysterious events by **contrasting** them with ordinary happenings.

You are going to use the account of the *Mary Celeste* as the basis for writing a mystery story. You have the facts as far as they are known but, to make it more exciting, you need to use your imagination to add some other details.

1 Make notes about:

Setting

Set your story in one or more of these settings:

- the *Dei Gratia*
- the *Mary Celeste*
- the offices of the British Admiralty in Gibraltar, where the inquiry takes place.

Plot

These are the main events of the story:

- the *Dei Gratia* comes across the *Mary Celeste*
- the captain and the second mate go aboard

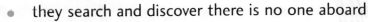

- they search and discover there is no one aboard
- they sail to Gibraltar
- the inquiry
- your own ending.

Characters

These are the main characters:

- the captain of the *Dei Gratia*
- the mate of the *Dei Gratia*
- other members of the *Dei Gratia*'s crew
- the people holding the inquiry.

But you can introduce any other character(s) you like.

2 Next, consider these questions and make some more notes.

- How will you begin your story? Will you begin at the inquiry, with the *Dei Gratia*'s crew telling the story of how they found the *Mary Celeste*, or will you begin on the *Dei Gratia* just before the doomed ship is spotted?
- How will you present the mystery to your reader?
  Are you going to write in the first person, as if you were one of the *Dei Gratia*'s crew?
  Think about how you would have felt and what you would have done. Perhaps you will write as if you were one of the people at the inquiry, listening to the events being told and deciding what really happened. Or you could write in the third person, as if you were not involved.
- How will you end your story? This is where you can really let your imagination work!
  Can you solve the mystery?
  Is someone going to tell the inquiry exactly what happened?
  Does one of the missing crew members suddenly appear?
  Did someone from a passing ship see what happened?

3 Plan your story, working out what is going to happen in each paragraph.

4 Write your first draft, revise and proofread it carefully, then think of an exciting title.

5 Write out your final copy.

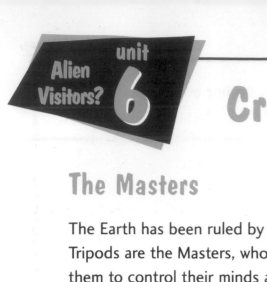
Creatures from Space

The Masters

The Earth has been ruled by the Tripods for many years. Inside the Tripods are the Masters, who keep humans in their power by 'capping' them to control their minds and bodies. Some people, including Will Parker, have managed to escape capping and have banded together to fight the Masters. Parker and two of his companions, all wearing false caps, have been taken into the Masters' city to be slaves. Here, Will describes his first sight of the Masters.

For all the discomfort and fatigue, and fears as to what might happen, the first impulse I had was to laugh. They were so grotesque! They stood much taller than a man, nearly twice as tall, and were broad in proportion. Their bodies were wider at the bottom than the top, four or five feet around I thought, but tapered upwards to something like a foot in circumference at the head. If it was a head, for there was no break in the continuity, no sign of a

neck. The next thing I noticed was that their bodies were supported not on two legs but three, these being thick but short. They had, matching them, three arms, or rather tentacles, issuing from a point about halfway up their bodies. And their eyes – I saw that there were three of those, too, set in a flattened triangle, one above and between the other, a foot or so below the crown. In colour the creatures were green, though I saw that the shades differed, some being dark, the green tinged with brown, and others quite pallid. That, and the fact that their heights varied to some extent, appeared to be the only means of telling one from another. I felt it was a poor one.

Later I was to discover that, as one grew accustomed to them, identification was easier than I had expected. The orifices which were their mouths, and nose, and ears, varied too – in size, in shape a little, and in their relationship with each other. They were connected by a pattern of wrinkles and creases which one learned to know and recognise. At first impact, though, they were faceless, almost completely uniform. It sent a shiver of quite a different fear down my spine when one of them, stopping before me, spoke.

from *The City of Gold and Lead* by John Christopher

Comprehension

A
1 Will experiences two sorts of fear. What is he frightened of?
2 Why do you think Will wanted to laugh when he first saw the Masters?
3 Make a list of the main physical differences between humans and the Masters.
4 Once he had become familiar with them, how could Will tell the Masters apart?
5 Write your own definition of each of the following words from the extract.
    a fatigue   b circumference
    c pallid   d orifices

Strange Plants

This is part of John Wyndham's story *The Day of the Triffids*, which tells how strange plants from outer space, called triffids, begin growing on Earth. At first, people do not realise just what they have growing in their gardens.

My introduction to a triffid came early. It so happened that we had one of the first in the locality growing in our garden. The plant was quite well developed before any of us bothered to notice it, for it had taken root along with a number of other casuals behind a bit of hedge that screened the rubbish heap. It wasn't doing any harm there, and it wasn't in anyone's way ...

Nobody, as far as I know, felt any misgivings or alarm about them then. I imagine that most people thought of them – when they thought of them at all – in much the same way as my father did.

I have a picture in my memory of him examining ours and puzzling over it at a time when it must have been about a year old ... My father leant over, peering at it through his horn-rimmed glasses, fingering its stalk, and blowing gently through his gingery moustache as was his habit when thoughtful. He inspected the straight stem, and the woody bole from which it sprang. He gave curious, if not very penetrative attention to the three small, bare sticks which grew up straight beside the stem.

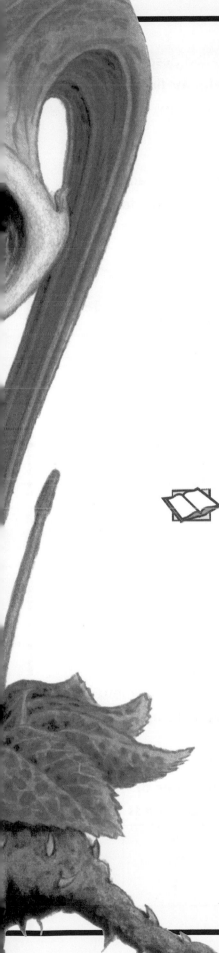

He smoothed the short sprays of leathery green leaves between his finger and thumb as if their texture might tell him something. Then he peered into the curious, funnel-like formation at the top of the stem, still puffing reflectively but inconclusively through his moustache. I remember the first time he lifted me up to look inside that conical cup and see the tightly-wrapped whorl within. It looked not unlike the new, close-rolled frond of a fern, emerging a couple of inches from a sticky mess in the base of the cup. I did not touch it, but I knew the stuff must be sticky because there were flies and other small insects struggling in it ...

And so the one in our garden continued its growth peacefully, as did thousands like it in neglected spots all over the world.

It was some time later that the first one picked up its roots and walked.

Comprehension

B 1 How do you think people felt when they first noticed triffids growing in their gardens?

2 At this point in the story, how does the writer want you to feel about triffids?

3 Write the conversation between two boys – Ajit and Tom – after Tom discovers a triffid growing in his garden.

C Look at *The City of Gold and Lead*.

1 Why do you think that John Christopher describes the Masters in such detail?

2 How does he want you to feel about them?

Look at *The Day of the Triffids*.

3 Why does John Wyndham at first make the triffids sound quite ordinary and nothing to be afraid of?

4 Why do you think he did not begin by saying that the triffids could walk?

Vocabulary

Using a thesaurus

The passages on pages 44–47 give very detailed descriptions of alien life forms. Remember, a **thesaurus** is very useful for finding exactly the right words for descriptive writing like this. It can also help you to avoid repeating yourself.

A Look at this space creature and make a list of words and phrases that you could use to describe it. Use your thesaurus to help you.

B In your mind, create an alien from space. It can be as strange as you like! Now write a detailed description, so that the reader can picture what it looks like. Use plenty of descriptive words and don't repeat yourself. Use your thesaurus to help you.

Spelling

Syllables

Spelling long words can be made easier if we divide them into **syllables**. Remember, syllables are the sound 'parts' that make up a word, and each syllable has a vowel sound. For example:

Word	Syllables	Number of vowel letters	Number of vowel sounds	Number of syllables
discomfort	dis-com-fort	3	3	3
continued	con-tin-ued	4	3	3
penetrative	pen-et-rat-ive	5	4	4

Learn the words in this activity using the 'look, say, cover, write, check' method.

A Here are some words that are commonly misspelled. Write them down and break each word into its syllables. Try using the syllables to help you learn the correct spelling.

1 especially   2 address   3 necessary

4 interesting   5 immediately   6 Wednesday

7 difficult   8 occasic   9 dangerous

B Look at the two passages on pages 44–47.

1 Copy six of the longest words, and break them into syllables.

2 Find the longest one-syllable word.

3 Find the word with the most syllables.

Grammar

'Helper' verbs

It is sometimes difficult to know when to use **'helper' verbs**, or auxiliary verbs. Never use a 'helper' verb with:

saw   did   came

Always use a 'helper' verb with:

seen   done   come

For example:

I <u>saw</u> a fox.   I told Dad I <u>had seen</u> a fox.

A Copy these sentences, choosing the correct verb to complete each one.

1 I <u>saw/seen</u> a scary film about aliens on TV last night.

2 It <u>come/came</u> on quite late.

3 My friend, Lee, had <u>came/come</u> for tea, so he stayed to watch the film.

4 He said he had <u>saw/seen</u> it before.

5 I <u>did/done</u> my best not to seem scared.

B Put each of these verbs into a sentence of your own. Think about whether it needs a 'helper' verb.

1 seen   2 did   3 come   4 came

Sentence construction

Writing a summary

A **summary** is a shorter version of a piece of writing, which contains only the essential information from the original passage. The first paragraph on page 44, is a summary of the story so far of *The City of Gold and Lead*.

A Read again the extract from *The City of Gold and Lead* on pages 44–45.

1 Copy about ten key words or short phrases from the passage.

2 Turn back to this page so you cannot see the passage. Using just the notes you have written, write a summary of the passage using no more than 60 words.

B Think of a story that you have read recently, or a television programme you have watched. Summarise what happened in the story or programme. First, note down the key parts, and then write your summary. Try to keep below 120 words.

Writing

Science fiction

Writing stories about what might happen in the future is called **science fiction**. Sometimes, science fiction stories predict things that actually happen and become 'science fact'! H G Wells wrote a book called *The First Men in the Moon* many years before humans actually landed there. Luckily for us, *The City of Gold and Lead* and *The Day of the Triffids* have not come true!

You are going to write a science fiction story of your own. Like any stories, science fiction stories need careful planning and a great deal of imagination. You need to think about:

Setting

Some science fiction stories are set here on Earth, others are set in different worlds. Think about whether your story will be set:

- on Earth – choose somewhere you are familiar with and can describe clearly
- on another planet or world – you can let your imagination take over and describe a really weird and wonderful place.

Characters

The kind of characters you have will depend on the setting you have chosen. You will probably need to include:

- one or more alien creatures – you need to describe them very carefully, so that your readers can imagine what they look like
- one or more human characters, who meet the alien(s).

Remember, if your story is set on Earth, the aliens have to be able to breathe and move around on Earth, or have special equipment that enables them to do this.

What is the aliens' reason for coming to Earth?

How do the humans feel about the aliens?

If your story is set on another planet, the human characters are likely to be astronauts and scientists and they will be the aliens!

Will the humans be able to breathe and move on the other planet?

Are the creatures there friendly or unfriendly?

What are the humans' feelings and intentions?

Plot

You must think very carefully about what is going to happen in your story, and this will depend on your characters and setting. Think about what would happen if:

- aliens came to Earth and were unfriendly
- aliens came to Earth and were friendly
- friendly aliens came to Earth but were greeted by unfriendly humans
- humans met unfriendly creatures on a planet which they visited
- humans met friendly creatures on a planet they visited.

Don't just have the humans and aliens meeting and fighting, which would be very boring. If they are hostile to each other, there should be a good reason, and you should give the reader an idea of how they feel.

Now plan and write your science fiction story.

The Ghost of Thomas Kempe

In Penelope Lively's *The Ghost of Thomas Kempe*, Mr and Mrs Harrison and their children, James and Helen, move into an old cottage across the road from an elderly widow called Mrs Verity. In the cottage, James becomes aware of the presence of Thomas Kempe, a seventeenth-century sorcerer who wants to make James his apprentice. Bert Ellison, the local handyman, believes James's story and agrees to help him get rid of the ghost.

He was rolling up the rug from the centre of the floor, and pushing back the table.

'What are you doing?' said James nervously.

'We've got to clear a place for the circle, haven't we? What would your mother say to the odd chalk mark on the floor, do you think?'

'I don't think she'd be very pleased.'

'Well, we'd better not go causing trouble, I suppose. We'll have to make do with paper and pencil, though it should be chalk, properly speaking.' He delved into his overall pocket, and brought out a pencil, and then an envelope and contents which he was about to tear into pieces when he looked more closely and said, 'No. That's my football coupon, I'll be wanting that.'

'I've got some paper,' said James.

'Let's have it then.'

Bert tore a sheet of paper into eight pieces, sat down at the table, and pencilled on each one a series of indecipherable marks and scrawls, breathing heavily as he did so.

'What do they mean?' said James.

'Ah,' said Bert, 'now you're asking me. I had them from my dad, to tell the truth. He did a bit in this line, from time to time. I couldn't exactly tell you what they mean, but they've been known to work, and that's a fact.'

He placed the eight pieces of paper in a circle in the centre of the floor, weighting each one down with a nail from his toolbox. In the middle of the circle he put the forked rowan stick, propped against a chair. Then he walked over to the curtains, peered up at the top of them, and said, 'Drat it, these has got some sort of modern nonsense. It's the old-fashioned kind we need.'

'What?' said James, bewildered.

'A curtain ring, son. We need a brass curtain ring. Can you fix us up with one of them?'

'I 'spect so,' said James. He bolted down the stairs, dashed into the sitting room, rummaged in his mother's work-drawer, found what he was looking for ...

Bert placed the curtain ring over the pointed end of the stick, so that it slipped down the fork. Then he stepped away from the circle, motioned James back with his hand, cleared his throat loudly and said, 'Thomas Kempe! Are you there?'

James, who had not expected such a direct approach, was startled ...

Nothing happened. Bert coughed, adjusted one of the pieces of paper and said, 'Enter the circle, and let us speak with you. Come!'

'What happens if he does?' whispered James.

'It'll do for him. The rowan, see. Rowan's no good for chaps like him. But you got to get him in there first.' Downstairs, a door banged, and somewhere outside Tim was barking.

'Thomas Kempe! I summon you!' said Bert severely. One of the pieces of paper lifted at the edge, as though examined by a curious breeze. There was a creak, that might or might not have been the shifting of ancient timbers. Bert said, in a murmur, 'He's biting! No doubt about it. This is where we got to go carefully. You've got to play them like a fish at this stage, see ... '

Down below, the front gate clicked and someone came up the path.

'Your mum?' said Bert.

'No,' said James. Footsteps are like voices, instantly known. 'It'll be someone collecting or something. Helen'll go.' He was staring at the rowan stick. Was it moving, quivering just a little?

'You have a word with him,' said Bert. 'After all, it's you seem to have set him off in the first place.'

The last time I did that, thought James, it didn't turn out very well ... With his eyes riveted on the stick (surely the ring twitched just then?) he said diffidently, 'Are you there?' The stick shook. One of the nails rolled off its piece of paper.

'Ah,' said Bert. 'Go on.'

'Please could I talk to you?' said James more confidently. A small fist of air wandered across the back of his neck and the stick shook again, nudging the back of the chair. Downstairs, the front door

Hello how are you? I'm fine thanks

opened and closed. There were voices in the hall – Helen and somebody else, but he hadn't time to listen.

'You're doing fine,' said Bert. 'Carry on like this and I'll be out of a job.'

'I wanted to ask you …' said James intensely, and the stick rubbed up and down again and the ring caught a strip of sunlight and flashed at him. The voices were louder.

'I wanted to ask if …' and then suddenly the voices were on the landing below and coming up the stairs and it was Helen and Mrs Verity and Mrs Verity was saying '… so if you don't mind dear I'll just pop up and have a word with him while he's here.' The stick fell over with a clatter. The curtains bellied out into the room as the window burst open under a roll of air pressure. Mrs Verity and Helen came in as Bert was kicking the stick hastily under the bed and sweeping up the pieces of paper in one hand.

Comprehension

A 1 What did Bert do instead of drawing with chalk on the floor?
2 From whom did Bert learn the 'indecipherable marks'?
3 What did James go downstairs to find?
4 Why did Bert want Thomas Kempe to enter the circle?
5 Who came into the room just as Bert was hiding the stick?

B 1 We are told that James 'nervously' asked Bert what he was doing.
Can you think of two reasons why James would be nervous?
2 Make a list of the things Bert needed to get rid of the ghost.
3 What does Bert mean when he says, 'You've got to play them like a fish at this stage'.
4 Find each of the following words in the passage and write a word or short phrase that the author could have used instead.

a indecipherable   b startled   c summon
d riveted   e diffidently   f wandered
g intensely   h bellied   i hastily

C How do you think the author wants her readers to feel as they read through the extract?
Think how you feel when:

- Bert is getting the room ready   ⟶ • Bert summons Thomas Kempe
- nothing happens   ⟶ • things begin to happen
- James begins to talk to Thomas Kempe ⟶ • voices are heard outside the room
- the door opens.

The Unexplained unit 7

Vocabulary

Our changing language

You have already seen how our language has **changed** over time, as new words are created and old words go out of use. Some words have been used for a very long time but have changed their meaning. For example, 'without' used to mean 'outside', but now it usually means 'not having'.

Other words have developed an extra, new meaning more recently, but still keep their original meaning, too. For example, 'gym' used to be used as an abbreviation for 'gymnastics', but now we usually use it to refer to a sports centre with equipment for getting fit.

Modern slang (non-standard English) often reverses the meaning of a word, so 'bad' might be used to mean 'good'.

A Copy this table and write the more modern meaning of each word.

Word	Original meaning	Modern meaning
cool	not very warm	
chill	cool down	
buggy	horse-drawn carriage	
rave	talk wildly	
flat	level surface	
keen	sharp	
club	an organisation	

New technologies add new words to our language. Many of the words already have other meanings. For example, 'surf' is a water sport, in which people ride the waves on a board but, now, the word 'surf' also means to 'ride' the Internet, skipping from page to page.

B Research and write down the new meaning of each of these words, which are used in computing and by people using the Internet.

1 web	2 hack	3 server
4 backbone	5 spam	6 flame
7 bookmarks	8 crash	9 newbie

Spelling

Roots, prefixes and suffixes

Remember, **roots**, **prefixes** and **suffixes** can help you to spell some words and may give you a clue about their meanings. For example:

'decipher' = to understand codes or secret writing

de = reverse or remove (from Latin)

cipher = secret writing, or code (from Arabic)

'bibliophile' = a lover of books

biblio = books (from Greek)

phile = to love (from Greek)

Many prefixes used in English originally came from other languages, but some are based on English words and are therefore easier to spell. For example, 'down' is a prefix for:

downbeat	downcast	downfall
downhill	downpour	downtrodden

A Write three words that begin with each of these English prefixes.

1 over   2 out   3 under

4 up   5 be   6 to

B Copy each group of words below and circle the common prefix, suffix or root in each group of words. What do you think it means? Use a dictionary to find the meaning of each word below and make a note of the language from which the common prefix/suffix/root came.

1 arachnaphobia hydrophobia   agoraphobia
  claustrophobia xenophobia

2 pressure   impress   pressurise   depress

3 antiseptic   antibiotic   antifreeze   antidote

4 domain   domestic   domicile

5 insomnia   somnambulism somnolent

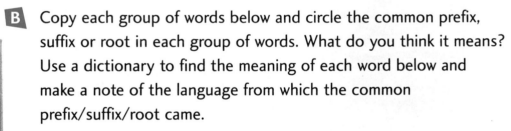

Grammar

Active and passive

Remember, if the action of the verb is done by the subject of the sentence, it is an **active verb** and an **active sentence**. If the subject of the sentence has the action of the verb done to it, we call it a **passive verb** and a **passive sentence**. For example:

Active sentence: Robin washed the dishes.

Passive sentence: The dishes were washed by Robin.

Sometimes, though, the sentence doesn't state who is doing the action. For example:

The paper <u>was torn</u> into pieces.

| subject | passive verb |

We know the action of the verb was done to the subject, but we don't know by whom. The sentence could have read:

The paper <u>was torn</u> into pieces by Bert.

A Write these passive sentences, concealing who or what did the action. The first has been done to help you.

1   The rug was rolled up by Bert.

     The rug was rolled up.

2   Bert was told the story about the ghost by James.

3   Eight pieces of paper were placed in a circle on the floor by Bert.

4   James was startled by the direct approach of Bert.

5   Bert was distracted by the voices in the hall.

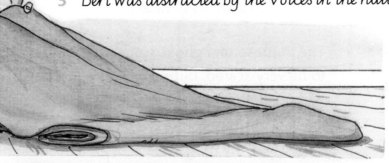

B Now rewrite each of the sentences from part A as active sentences. The first one has been done to help you.

1   Bert rolled up the rug.

Punctuation

Direct speech

Remember, when punctuating **direct speech**, begin a new line each time a new person starts to speak. Also, remember that the punctuation mark at the end of a piece of dialogue should always be inside the final speech marks. For example:

"What are you doing?" asked James nervously.

"I've got some paper," said James.

A Copy these sentences, adding the missing speech marks.

1 Do you believe in ghosts? asked James.

2 No way! his friend replied, without even looking up.

3 I think I do, said James.

4 Tom was busy and didn't want to talk, but added, OK then.

5 You're not listening to me, snapped James.

B Copy this passage, adding the missing punctuation and setting it out correctly.

I have never seen a ghost said Tom and I don't know anyone who has But that doesn't mean ghosts can't exist said James I agree replied Tom but nobody has ever found any evidence for ghosts Many people talk about seeing ghosts but they are usually people who have a very vivid imagination Quietly James said perhaps you'd like to come and stay in my room one night and then you'll see for yourself!

Writing

Ghost stories

The purpose of a **ghost story** is to frighten the reader. It isn't pleasant to be very scared, but people do enjoy being just a little bit frightened! Writers of ghost stories create a sense of excitement and mystery by building **suspense**.

One way of creating a sense of excitement and mystery in a ghost story is to contrast ordinary things with very unusual things. This can be done with fairly small details. For example, in the passage from *The Ghost of Thomas Kempe*, the following contrasts are made:

	Ordinary	Unusual
Characters	Bert, James, Helen, Mrs Verity	Thomas Kempe
Setting	the village James's house	the atmosphere in James's room
Plot	Bert finding his football coupon someone coming to the house the front door opening and closing Mrs Verity and Helen coming into the room	marks and scrawls on the paper pieces of paper arranged in a circle the rowan stick the breeze on James's neck the window bursting open

The suspense is built up because we do not know if Bert and James will succeed in getting Thomas Kempe to appear before they are interrupted. The author contrasts the strange happenings in James's bedroom and the ordinary life going on downstairs.

A Imagine you are the ghost of Thomas Kempe. You are in the room all the time Bert and James are planning to lure you into the circle and get rid of you. Write about how you feel and what you think of what they are doing.

B Write your own ghost story. To create a sense of excitement and mystery, use the same method of contrasting the ordinary with the unusual as in *The Ghost of Thomas Kempe*. Make a list like the one above of the 'ordinary' and the 'unusual' aspects of your story. Brainstorm your ideas and remember to:

- make notes on setting, characters and plot (include a good beginning and ending)
- work out what is going to happen in each paragraph
- think of an interesting title
- write a first draft
- proofread and revise your first draft
- neatly write out your final copy.

George

Who played with a Dangerous Toy, and suffered a
Catastrophe of considerable Dimensions.

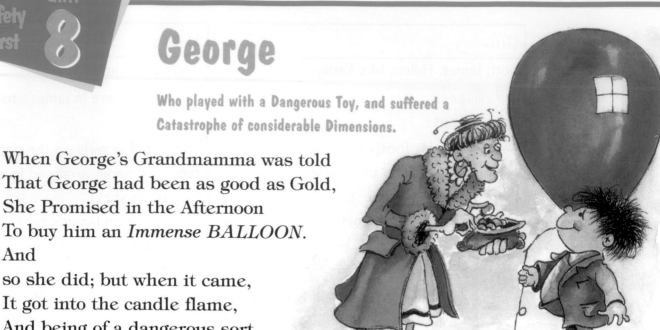

When George's Grandmamma was told
That George had been as good as Gold,
She Promised in the Afternoon
To buy him an *Immense BALLOON*.
And
so she did; but when it came,
It got into the candle flame,
And being of a dangerous sort
Exploded
with a loud report!
The Lights went out! The Windows broke!
The Room was filled with reeking smoke.
And in the darkness shrieks and yells
Were mingled with Electric Bells,
And falling masonry and groans,
And crunching, as of broken bones,
And dreadful shrieks, when, worst of all,
The House itself began to fall!
It tottered, shuddering to and fro,
Then crashed into the street below –
Which happened to be Savile Row.
When Help arrived, among the Dead

Were
Cousin Mary,
Little Fred,
The Footmen
(both of them),
The Groom,
The man that cleaned the Billiard-Room,
The Chaplain, and
The Still-Room Maid.

And I am dreadfully afraid
That Monsieur Champignon, the Chef,
Will now be
permanently deaf –
And both his
Aides
are much the same
While George, who was in part to blame,
Received, you will regret to hear,
A nasty lump
behind the ear.

MORAL
The moral is that little Boys
Should not be given dangerous Toys.

by Hilaire Belloc

61

Comprehension **A** 1 Who gave George the balloon?
2 Why did she give it to him?
3 How did the balloon come to cause so much damage?
4 List five things that happened when the balloon exploded.
5 What lesson is the poem teaching?

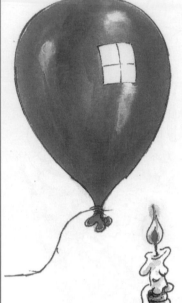

B Explain the meaning of the following words and phrases from the poem.

1 good as Gold   2 immense
3 a loud report   4 reeking
5 permanently   6 moral

C 1 Write some sentences to say what you think of the poem. Do you find it funny? Sad? Frightening? Why?
2 What do you think the poet wanted people to feel when they read the poem?

Vocabulary

Proverbs and idioms

Remember, **proverbs** are well-known, wise sayings. For example:
    There's no smoke without fire.
This means that small signs of trouble are usually caused by a bigger problem that is yet to be discovered.

A 1 Write a sentence to explain the meaning of each proverb.
  a A friend in need is a friend indeed.
  b As well to be hanged for a sheep as a lamb.
  c One good turn deserves another.
  d Least said, soonest mended.

2 Below are four proverbs from Africa. Briefly explain what you think each one means.
  a Wearing tusks is no trouble for the elephant.
  b Knead your clay while it is still wet.
  c A blind man should not pick up a stick; it might be a snake.

Remember, **idioms** are short phrases which mean something quite different from what might be expected. For example:

George had been <u>as good as gold</u>.

'As good as gold' means 'very good'.

B 1 Match each of the idioms with its correct meaning from the box. Write down the correct meaning of each idiom.

a	head in the clouds
b	beating about the bush
c	beside myself
d	the apple of his/her eye
e	down in the mouth
f	get cold feet

someone he/she especially loves

overwhelmed with strong emotion

in low spirits

lose courage

not getting to the point

day-dreaming

2 Complete each idiom below with an ending from the box.

your sleeve
a new leaf
the horns
the cold shoulder
a molehill

a make a mountain out of _____

b give somebody _____

c wear your heart on _____

d take the bull by _____

e turn over _____

3 Choose four idioms from questions 1 and 2 and use them in sentences of your own.

Spelling

Mnemonics

Mnemonics (pronounced 'nemonics') are short phrases or rhymes that help us to remember things. Some mnemonics can help you to remember how to spell difficult or confusing words. For example:

catastrophe   "The <u>cat</u> was in <u>a strop</u>," <u>he</u> said.

'Catastrophe' is a difficult word to spell, and this mnemonic helps you to remember the letters and their order.

A Copy the mnemonics below. In each one, underline the word that the mnemonic helps us to spell correctly. Use the mnemonics to learn how to spell the eight words.

1   an *island* is land surrounded by water.

2   Never end with a *friend* on Friday.

3   Without a 'g', *grammar* can be spelt backwards.

4   *Bought* means to buy; *brought* means to bring.

5   Sorry you're too late for any *chocolate*.

6   In no century is murder an *innocent* crime.

7   Lighten *lightning* by dropping the 'e'.

8   Miss Pell can't spell *misspell*.

B Create mnemonics for these tricky words from the poem 'George', or choose some other words that you particularly want to learn.

1 dangerous	2 nasty	3 necessary
4 shriek	5 permanent	6 immense

Grammar

Verbs

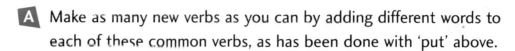

Adding a word or two to a common **verb** can make new meanings.
For example:

I <u>put</u> the mug on the table.

'Put' is a common verb. If we add other small words, we can make 'put'
have different meanings. For example:

I <u>put out</u> the fire.

I <u>put on</u> my clothes.

I <u>put off</u> doing my homework until the weekend.

I <u>put back</u> the book I had taken off the shelf.

A Make as many new verbs as you can by adding different words to
each of these common verbs, as has been done with 'put' above.

1 *get*   2 *give*   3 *make*   4 *let*

B 1 In each sentence below, underline the new verbs that have
been made by adding a word or two to a common verb.
The first one has been done to help you.

a *I had to <u>make up</u> a story to explain why I was late home.*

b *At the meeting, she <u>put forward</u> an idea.*

c *Those vandals were lucky to <u>get off</u> with a caution.*

d *Mum has <u>sent off</u> for a brochure.*

e *He <u>took</u> a week <u>off</u> to <u>get over</u> the operation.*

f *My sister tries to <u>get at</u> me all the time.*

g *I'm going to <u>go in</u> for a competition.*

h *I don't want to <u>fall out</u> with my best friend.*

i *We are going to Wales for the weekend to <u>get away</u>
from it all.*

2 For each phrase you underlined in question 1, write another
word or phrase that could be used instead. The first one has
been done to help you.

a *I had to invent a story to explain why I was late home.*

Sentence construction

Adjective clauses

Remember, an **adjective clause** tells us more about a noun or pronoun in the main clause. For example:

He burst the balloon which Grandmamma had bought him.

| main clause | | adjective clause, telling us more about the balloon |

Adjective clauses begin with:
- 'who' – only when the noun or pronoun is a person
- 'which' or 'that' – always when the noun or pronoun is an animal or object; sometimes when the noun or pronoun is a person.

A Copy the sentences below, using 'who' or 'which' to join the clauses.

1 What happened to the balloon _which_ George put too close to the candle?

2 It was George's kindly old grandmamma _who_ had given him the balloon.

3 It was a huge explosion _which_ broke the windows.

4 Most of the people _who_ were killed by the explosion were servants.

5 George was normally the sort of boy _who_ behaved well.

B Add an adjective clause to each of these main clauses to make a sentence.

1 In the billiard room was the man _who cleaned the billiard_.

2 Was it a candle _which had was a big flame_?

3 The explosion only slightly injured George, _who had made the explosion_.

4 The fire brigade were shocked by the scene _which was dramatik_.

5 Hilaire Belloc is a famous poet, _who is 60 years old_.

Writing

Humorous poems

The poem 'George' by Hilaire Belloc is a **humorous poem** of the sort called 'cautionary tales', which usually have a warning moral (message). Through the actions of the characters, the reader learns a valuable lesson. Dreadful things often happen in this sort of poem, but they are written in such a way that we find them funny.

A Write your own cautionary tale with a moral. You can use your own ideas or one of the following starting points.

Lesson: Never play near water.

Young Sam was always very fond
Of playing near a murky pond.
His mother warned him every day
He didn't listen, sad to say!

Lesson: Always brush your teeth night and morning.

Any food which tasted sweet
Was what Camilla liked to eat.
She didn't heed the dentist's warning
To brush her teeth both night and morning!

B Use the library to find out more about Hilaire Belloc and his poems. He wrote many cautionary tales. See if you can find and read some of them. Decide which one you like best.

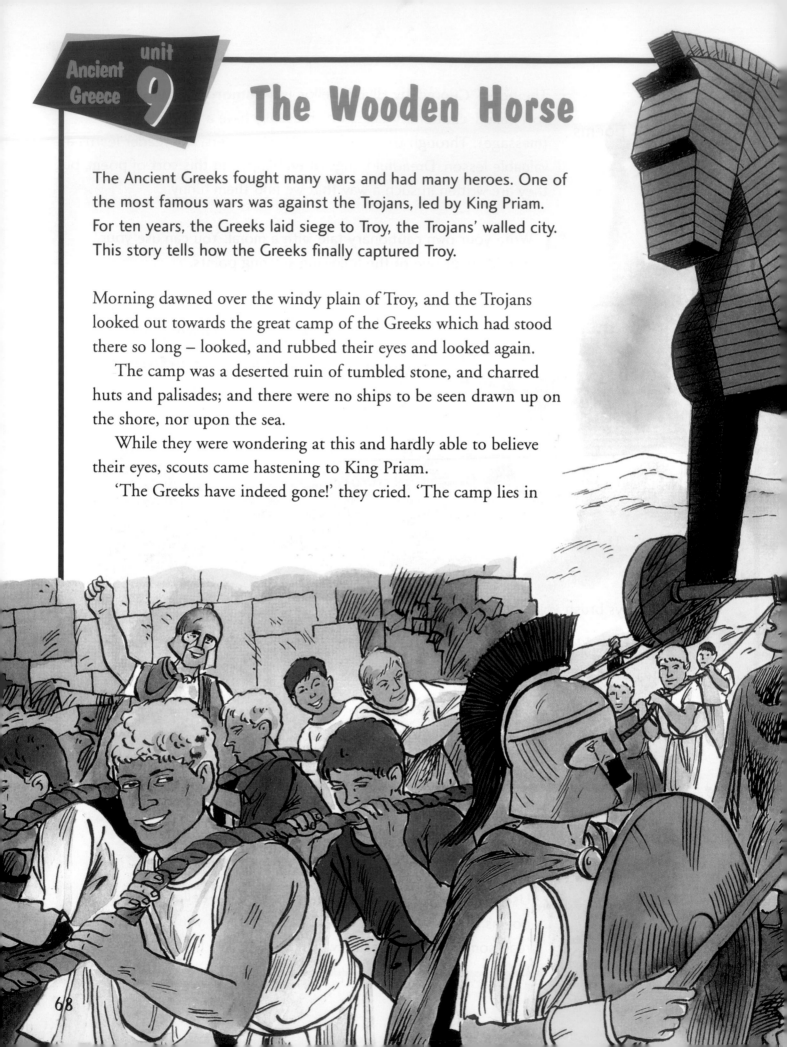

The Wooden Horse

The Ancient Greeks fought many wars and had many heroes. One of the most famous wars was against the Trojans, led by King Priam. For ten years, the Greeks laid siege to Troy, the Trojans' walled city. This story tells how the Greeks finally captured Troy.

Morning dawned over the windy plain of Troy, and the Trojans looked out towards the great camp of the Greeks which had stood there so long – looked, and rubbed their eyes and looked again.

The camp was a deserted ruin of tumbled stone, and charred huts and palisades; and there were no ships to be seen drawn up on the shore, nor upon the sea.

While they were wondering at this and hardly able to believe their eyes, scouts came hastening to King Priam.

'The Greeks have indeed gone!' they cried. 'The camp lies in

ashes; there is not a man, not a ship to be seen. But there stands in the midst of the ruins a great Wooden Horse the like of which we have never seen.'

Then the gates of Troy were flung open and out poured young and old, laughing and shouting in their joy that the Greeks were gone at last. Priam led the way with Queen Hecuba and their only surviving son Polites and their daughters Cassandra and Polyxena; and they came to the ruins and stood gazing at the great Wooden Horse.

And now they could see letters of gold inscribed on the Horse's side:

FOR THEIR RETURN HOME, THE GREEKS DEDICATE THIS THANK-OFFERING TO ATHENA

At once a great argument broke out among the Trojans as to what should be done with the Horse.

'It is a gift to Athena,' cried one chief, 'so let us take it into Troy and place it in her temple!'

'No, no!' cried another, 'rather let us fling it into the sea!'

The arguments grew fierce: many wished to destroy it, but more to keep it as a memorial of the war – and Priam favoured this course.

Then Laocoon the priest, a man of violent temper who had already insulted Poseidon the Immortal Lord of the Sea by failing to offer him his due sacrifices, rushed up crying:

'Wretched men, are you mad? Do you not realise that the Greeks have made this? May it not be some cunning engine devised by that evil creature Odysseus to break down our walls or spy into our houses. There is something guileful about it, I am certain, and I warn you, Trojans, not to trust this horse. Whatever it is, I fear the Greeks most when they make us gifts!'

And so they argued amongst themselves, but eventually they dragged the horse inside the city walls and had a great celebration with much drinking and merry-making. At last, all the Trojans fell into a deep sleep.

Not a sound of song or of revelry broke the stillness of the night, not even the baying of a dog was to be heard, but perfect silence reigned as if Night held her breath, awaiting the sudden outbreak of the noise of war and death.

Through that silence the Greek fleet stole back to the beaches; for on the mound which marked Achilles' tomb a great fire burned, kindled by Simon. And from Helen's window the light shone out so that the Greeks drew nearer and nearer to Troy, silent and sure, stealing through the early night to be there before the moon rose.

And when the first silvery beams came stealing over the black shape of distant Ida, Odysseus gave the word, and Epeius undid the bolt and opened the door beneath the belly of the Wooden Horse. In his eager haste Echion sprang out before the ladder was ready, and the fall killed him. But the other heroes climbed down in safety, stole through the silent streets, killed what sleepy sentinels there were on watch and opened the gates of Troy to Agamemnon and the armies of Greece.

from *The Tale of Troy* by Roger Lancelyn Green

GLOSSARY
Athena Greek goddess of wisdom
palisades fences
sentinels sentries

Comprehension **A** 1 Who was the King of Troy?
2 Who tried to persuade the Trojans to destroy the Horse?
3 What did they do with the Horse?
4 What did the Greeks do while the people of Troy slept?

B 1 How do you think:
a the Trojans felt when they saw that the Greeks had gone?
b the Greek heroes felt as they waited inside the Horse?
c the Trojans felt when they awoke to find the Greeks inside the city?
2 From this myth, we get the proverb 'Beware of Greeks bearing gifts.' What do you think this proverb means?
3 Find the following words and phrases in the passage and explain them in your own words.
a charred   b inscribed
c memorial of war   d insulted
e cunning engine   f revelry
g perfect silence reigned   h stealing

C Summarise the story by listing the main points of the plot.

The Caribbean unit **9**

70

 Vocabulary

Anagrams

Anagrams are made by rearranging the letters of a word or phrase to make a new word or phrase. For example:

horse – shore

the morse code – here come dots

A See if you can solve the following anagrams by rearranging the letters of each word to match the clue.

1 *wrote* – tall part of a castle

2 *otry* – ancient city

3 *ports* – competitive physical activity

4 *earn* – antonym of 'far'

5 *see pal* – The Greeks attacked when the Trojans were _____.

6 *paws* – a stinging insect

7 *softer* – a large wooded area

8 *earth* – an important organ in the body

9 *groan* – a large musical instrument

10 *disease* – somewhere you might go swimming and

make sandcastles

B Make up some anagrams from words from the story. Think of a simple clue for each, then challenge your friends to solve them.

Spelling

Unstressed vowels

Remember, **unstressed vowels** are vowels which we either do not sound, or don't sound very distinctly, as we speak. Unstressed vowels can cause spelling problems because it is easy to forget them and miss them out. For example:

scouts came <u>hastening</u> to King Priam

'Hastening' sounds like 'hastning' because the 'e' is an unstressed vowel.

A Copy these words. Circle the unstressed vowels.

1 fattening	2 stationary	3 separate
4 parliament	5 ordinary	6 secretary
7 jewellery	8 mathematics	9 interest

B Write down six more words that have unstressed vowels.

Hint 1: there are two in the passage.

Hint 2: think of the names of the days and months.

Hint 3: think of words from the same word family as those in part A.

Grammar

Simple verb tenses

The present and past tenses can usually be written a different way using a **helper verb**, e.g. 'She <u>is</u> jumping'.

Remember, there are three **simple verb tenses** – past, present and future. For example:

Verb family	Past tense	Present tense	Future tense
to jump	she jumped	she jumps	she will jump

Notice that the future tense verb needs a 'helper', or auxiliary, verb.

A Copy and complete this table.

Verb family	Past tense	Present tense	Future tense
to walk	she walked	she walks	she will walk
to shout	they _____	they _____	they _____ _____
to throw	he _____	he _____	he _____ _____
to fall	I _____	I _____	I _____ _____
to swim	we _____	we _____	we _____ _____
to fight	you _____	you _____	you _____ _____
to think	she _____	she _____	she _____ _____
to run	it _____	it _____	it _____ _____

Be careful! Some of these verbs are **irregular** – they change rather than having the suffix 'ed' or 'ing' added.

B Rewrite these sentences in the past tense.

1 The Greeks hide in the horse.

2 Everyone in the city celebrates.

3 They feel such relief.

4 The crowd drags the wooden horse into the city.

5 Only the priest suspects a trick.

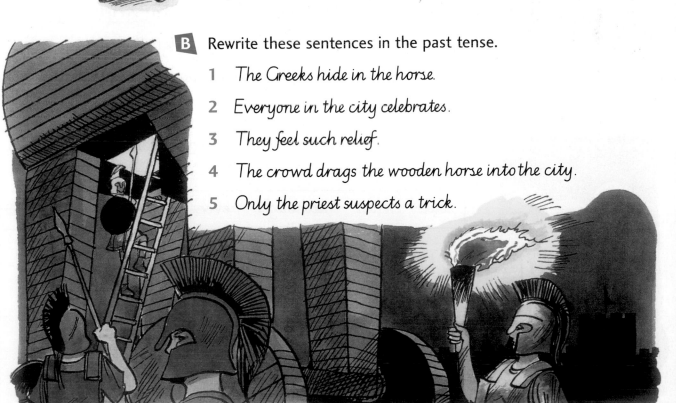

Sentence construction

Adverb clauses

Remember, **adverbs** tell us how, when or where the action of a verb takes place.

Remember, an adjective clause tells us more about a noun or pronoun in the main clause. For example:

The Trojans looked out towards the Greek camp, *which* had stood there so long.

| main clause | | adjective clause, telling us more about the camp |

Adjective clauses begin with 'who', 'which' or 'that'.

An **adverb clause** tells us more about a <u>verb</u> in the main clause. For example:

They cheered loudly *because* they thought the Greeks had given up.

| main clause | | adverb clause, telling us more about <u>why</u> they cheered |

Adverb clauses begin with conjunctions.

A Copy these sentences. Underline the adverb clause in each, and draw a ring around the verb that the adverb clause tells us more about.

1   The Trojans ran out as soon as they saw the wooden horse.

2   They pulled it to the gate although it was very heavy.

3   It became stuck when they tried to pull it through the gate.

4   The horse wouldn't fit because the gate was too narrow.

B Add an adverb clause to each of these main clauses to make an interesting sentence. Choose a conjunction from the box to begin each adverb clause.

| but | when | although | even | though | because | so |

1   The heroes were sitting inside the horse _____ .

2   The Greek ships returned to the harbour _____ .

3   In Troy, everyone was sleeping _____ .

Writing

A reading journal

A **reading journal** is an excellent way to keep a record of the books and stories you read. In a reading journal, it is a good idea to record:

- the title of the story or book
- the author
- the date
- a brief summary of the plot
- your opinion of the book, with reasons.

It is important to keep a record of all the books and stories you read, not just the ones you enjoyed. If you didn't enjoy something you have read, make a note of your reasons.

Below is an entry in a reading journal for the passage on pages 68–70

TITLE: *The Tale of Troy*

AUTHOR: *Roger Lancelyn Green*

DATE: *March 2000*

PLOT: This is one episode in a book about the Trojan War. The Greeks have been camping outside Troy for 10 years, trying to conquer the city. One day, the Greeks pretend to leave and the Trojans assume they have won the war. The Greeks have left a huge wooden horse outside the city, and the Trojans drag it inside before celebrating their victory. While the Trojans are asleep, Greek heroes, who have been hiding in the horse, emerge and open the city gates to let in the rest of the Greek army, which had sneaked back.

WHAT I THOUGHT OF IT: This was an exciting story. I was sure the Greeks had not just given up and sailed away but I did not guess they were hiding in the horse. I was sorry that the Trojans were fooled and that the Greeks finally won by using trickery, but it was a clever plan.

Begin your own reading journal by writing about a book or story you have read recently.

Cliffs Under Attack

One way in which a writer can keep the reader's interest is to provide clues so that the reader can predict what might happen. Sometimes, a reader's prediction can be totally wrong, as the author puts something unexpected in the story. Sometimes, a reader may predict several things, only some of which happen. This makes the story more exciting.

Read the beginning of *The Iron Man* by Ted Hughes. Stop each time you are asked a question about what might happen next. Write:

• what you think might happen

• what clues you used to make your prediction.

Then read on to see if you are right.

The Iron Man came to the top of the cliff.

How far had he walked? Nobody knows. Where had he come from? Nobody knows. How was he made? Nobody knows.

Taller than a house, the Iron Man stood at the top of the cliff, on the very brink, in the darkness.

The wind sang through his iron fingers. His great iron head, shaped like a dustbin but as big as a bedroom, slowly turned to the right, slowly turned to the left. His iron ears turned, this way, that way. He was hearing the sea. His eyes, like headlamps, glowed white, then red, then infra-red, searching the sea. Never before had the Iron Man seen the sea.

He swayed in the strong wind that pressed against his back. He swayed forward, on the brink of the high cliff.

---

1 What do you think happens next?

And his right foot, his enormous iron right foot, lifted – up, out, into space, and the Iron Man stepped forward, off the cliff, into nothingness.

CRRRAAAASSSSSSH!

Down the cliff the Iron Man came toppling, head over heels.

CRASH!

CRASH!

CRASH!

From rock to rock, snag to snag, tumbling slowly. And as he crashed and crashed and crashed ...

 2 What do you think happened to the Iron Man as he crashed down the cliff?

His iron legs fell off.

His iron arms broke off, and the hands broke off the arms.

His great iron ears fell off and his eyes fell out.

His great iron head fell off.

All the separate pieces tumbled, scattered, crashing, bumping, clanging, down on to the rocky beach far below.

A few rocks tumbled with him.

Then

Silence.

Only the sound of the sea, chewing away at the edge of the rocky beach, where the bits and pieces of the Iron Man lay scattered far and wide, silent and unmoving.

Only one of the iron hands, lying beside an old, sand-logged washed-up seaman's boot, waved its fingers for a minute, like a crab on its back. Then it lay still.

While the stars went on wheeling through the sky and the wind went on tugging at the grass on the cliff-top and the sea went on boiling and booming.

Nobody knew the Iron Man had fallen.

3 Do you think this is the end of the Iron Man?

Night passed.

Just before dawn, as the darkness grew blue and the shapes of the rocks separated from each other, two seagulls flew crying over the rocks. They landed on a patch of sand. They had two chicks in a nest on the cliff. Now they were searching for food.

One of the seagulls flew up – Aaaaaark! He had seen something. He glided low over the sharp rocks. He landed and picked something up. Something shiny, round and hard.

 4 What do you think the seagull has found?

It was one of the Iron Man's eyes. He brought it back to his mate. They both looked at this strange thing. And the eye looked at them. It rolled from side to side looking first at one gull, then at the other. The gulls, peering at it, thought it was a strange kind of clam, peeping at them from its shell.

Then the other gull flew up, wheeled around and landed and picked up something. Some awkward, heavy thing. The gull flew low and slowly, dragging the heavy thing. Finally, the gull dropped it beside the eye. This new thing had five legs. It moved. The gulls thought it was a strange kind of crab. They thought they had found a strange crab and a strange clam.

 5 What do you think the other gull has found?

They did not know they had found the Iron Man's eye and the Iron Man's right hand.

But as soon as the eye and the hand got together the eye looked at the hand. Its light glowed blue. The hand stood up on three fingers and its thumb, and craned its forefinger like a long nose. It felt around. It touched the eye. Gleefully it picked up the eye, and tucked it under its middle finger.

The eye peered out, between the forefinger and the thumb. Now the hand could see.

 6 What do you think the eye and the hand do now?

Vocabulary

Word games

As well as being fun, **word games** can help you to learn tricky spellings and to increase your vocabulary.

A Copy the word grid below. Write the answers to the clues in the correct rows of the grid. The answers are all words that contain either a 'soft' sounding 'c' (that sounds like the 's' in 'sun') or a 'soft' sounding 'g' (that sounds like the 'j' in 'job'). If your answers are correct, the letters in the blue boxes will make a word.

1 the party after a wedding

2 the last month of the year

3 very, very good

4 getting your own back

5 middle

6 a small house in the country

7 the American term for rubbish

8 a tall animal with a long neck

9 a very large town

B Devise a similar puzzle for 'ough' words (e.g. cough, dough).

Spelling

Unstressed letters

It is important to learn words with unstressed vowels and consonants because they are difficult to spell!

Remember, **unstressed vowels** are vowels which we either do not sound, or do not sound very distinctly, as we speak. For example:

a reader may predict several things

'several' sounds like 'sevral' because the 'e' is an unstressed vowel.

Some words have **unstressed consonants**. For example:

His great iron head was shaped like a dustbin.

'iron' sounds like 'ion' because the 'r' is an unstressed consonant and 'dustbin' sounds like 'dusbin' because the 't' is an unstressed consonant.

A Copy these words. Circle the unstressed vowels or consonants.

1 cupboard   2 history   3 happening

4 shepherd   5 miniature   6 dictionary

7 different   8 postpone   9 environment

10 government   11 medicine   12 raspberry

Remember, a **mnemonic** is a short phrase or rhyme to help you remember a spelling.

B 1 Choose four of the hardest words from part A and write a mnemonic for each one, to help you remember how to spell it.

2 Look carefully at the words with unstressed consonants. Write a sentence explaining what causes these consonants to be unstressed.

3 Look back through some of your own writing, or a book you have been reading, and list some more words that have unstressed letters.

Grammar

Idiom origins

Remember, **expressions** are common sayings, and **idioms** are expressions that have a different meaning to what they actually say. It is interesting to research why and when expressions were first used. For example:

They made him <u>carry the can</u>.

The idiom 'to carry the can' means to be reluctantly responsible for something. There are two possible origins:

* Miners took it in turns to <u>carry the can</u> of explosives into the mine each morning.

* Soldiers took it in turns to <u>carry the can</u> to empty the toilet each morning!

It's easy to see how this expression started!

A For each idiom below, choose from the box the correct clue about its origin. Write down the clues.

- in Roman times, soldiers used to have the names of their sweethearts stitched onto the sleeves of their uniforms
- the position the players take at the start of a marbles competition
- long ago, the mercury used in hat-making made hat-makers behave strangely
- when buying a horse, the only way to tell if the owner is telling the truth about the horse's age is to look at its teeth
- an organ makes the loudest noise when the stops are pulled out
- when a soldier was thrown out of the army, a drummer would play as he left
- a nineteenth-century Australian boxer, Larry Foley, was a jolly character
- in Scottish dialect, 'argle' means 'to haggle.'
- a form of torture
- at the end of a battle at sea, victorious ships still had their flags flying

1 straight from the horse's mouth

2 as mad as a hatter

3 knuckle down

4 wear your heart on your sleeve

5 drummed out

6 as happy as Larry

7 argy-bargy

8 haul over the coals

9 with flying colours

10 pull out all the stops

B Choose four of the expressions from part A and put them into sentences of your own.

Punctuation

Practising punctuation

Writing

Book reviews

A Copy these sentences, adding the missing punctuation marks and capital letters.

1 i think the iron man is a brilliant book said marek

2 i dont responded mike its a terrible book

3 youre stupid snapped marek rudely its one of the greatest childrens books ever written

4 says who asked mike in a rather surly manner

5 says me retorted marek and a few million other people

B Finish the conversation begun in part A, remembering to begin a new line each time the speaker changes.

The purpose of a **book review** is to help other people to decide whether they would like to read it.

A book review for a **fiction** book should include:

1 the book title

2 the author's name

3 the type of book – whether it is a novel, short story, poetry, etc.

4 the age of the audience the book is written for – very young children, juniors, teenagers, etc.

5 a brief summary of the story – without giving away the ending!

6 the personal opinion of the reviewer – whether they enjoyed the book, their reasons for enjoying/not enjoying it, whether it was interesting, exciting, frightening, etc.

A book review for a **non-fiction** book should include items 1 to 4 above, plus:

5 a brief summary of what sort of information is in the book

6 a short explanation of how the information is presented – maps, charts, diagrams, photographs, etc.

7 your opinion about how easy the text is to follow, how effectively the information is presented and how useful the book is.

A Read this book review, then answer the questions below.

The Iron Man by Ted Hughes is a modern fairy story that can be enjoyed by children and adults alike. The main character is the Iron Man, a metal giant. Nobody knows where he came from or how he was made. Hughes imaginatively relates the Iron Man's travels. Various attempts are made to destroy the Iron Man, who frightens everyone he sees, but hatred turns into pleas for help when a space-bat-angel-dragon arrives. Will the Iron Man be able to save the world?

The book is beautifully written and keeps you turning the pages until the very end.

1 What is the name of the book being reviewed?
2 Who is the author?
3 What type of book is it?
4 Which audience do you think the book was written for?
5 What does the reviewer think of the book?
6 Briefly summarise in your own words the plot of the passage on pages 76–78.

B You are going to write your own book review. Follow the following steps carefully.
1 Choose a book which you have recently read and enjoyed.
2 Depending on whether the book is fiction or non-fiction, make sure your review includes all the items listed in the teaching box on page 82.

The Legend of Alderley

At dawn one still October day in the long ago of the world, across the hill of Alderley, a farmer from Mobberley was riding to Macclesfield fair.

The morning was dull, but mild; light mists bedimmed his way; the woods were hushed; the day promised fine. The farmer was in good spirits, and he let his horse, a milk-white mare, set her own pace, for he wanted her to arrive fresh for the market. A rich man would walk back to Mobberley that night.

So, his mind in the town while he was yet on the hill, the farmer drew near to the place known as Thieves' Hole. And there the horse stood still and would answer to neither spur nor rein. The spur and the rein she understood, and her master's stern command, but the eyes that held her were stronger than all these.

In the middle of the path, where surely there had been no one, was an old man, tall, with long hair and beard. "You go to sell this mare," he said. "I come here to buy. What is your price?"

But the farmer wished to sell only at the market, where he would have a choice of many offers, so he rudely bade the stranger quit the path and let him through, for if he stayed longer he would be late to the fair.

"Then go your way," said the old man. "None will buy. And I shall await you here at sunset."

The next moment he was gone, and the farmer could not tell how or where.

The day was warm, and the tavern cool, and all who saw the mare agreed that she was a splendid animal, the pride of Cheshire, a queen among horses; and everyone said that there was no finer beast in the town. But no one offered to buy. A sour-eyed farmer rode out of Macclesfield at the end of the day.

Near Thieves' Hole the mare stopped: the stranger was there.

Thinking any price was better than none, the farmer agreed to sell. "How much will you give?" he said.

"Enough. Now come with me."

By Seven Firs and Goldenstone they went, to Stormy Point and Saddlebole. And they halted before a great rock embedded in the hillside. The old man lifted his staff and lightly touched the rock, and it split with the noise of thunder.

At this, the farmer toppled from his plunging horse and, on his knees, begged the other to have mercy on him and let him go his way unharmed. The horse should stay; he did not want her. Only spare his life, that was enough.

The wizard, for such he was, commanded the farmer to rise. "I promise you safe conduct," he said. "Do not be afraid, for living wonders you shall see here."

Beyond the rock stood a pair of iron gates. These the wizard opened, and took the farmer and the horse down a narrow tunnel deep into the hill. A light, subdued but beautiful, marked their way. The passage ended, and they stepped into a cave, and there a wondrous sight met the farmer's eyes – a hundred and forty knights in silver armour, and by the side of all but one a milk-white mare.

"Here they lie in enchanted sleep," said the wizard, "until the day will come – and come it will – when England shall be in direst peril, and England's mothers weep. Then out from the hill these must ride and, in battle thrice lost, thrice won, upon the plain, drive the enemy into the sea."

The farmer, dumb with awe, turned with the wizard into a further cavern, and here mounds of gold and silver and precious stones lay strewn along the ground.

"Take what you can carry in payment for the horse."

And when the farmer had crammed his pockets (ample as his lands!), his shirt, and his fists with jewels, the wizard hurried him up the long tunnel and thrust him out of the gates. The farmer stumbled, the thunder rolled, he looked, and there was only the rock above him. He was alone on the hill, near Stormy Point. The broad full moon was up, and it was night.

And although in later years he tried to find the place, neither he nor any after him ever saw the iron gates again.

from *The Weirdstone of Brisingamen* by Alan Garner

Comprehension

A 1 Why didn't the farmer want to sell the mare to the old man?
2 What was strange about what happened at Macclesfield fair?
3 What did the farmer see in the cave?
4 How did the wizard pay him for the horse?
5 Write, in your own words, why the sleeping knights would one day awake and come out of the cave.

B 1 Explain what you think the author means by each of the following phrases.
  a A rich man would walk back to Mobberley that night.
  b his mind in the town while he was yet on the hill
  c would answer to neither spur nor reign
  d I promise you safe conduct
  e in direst peril
2 How did the horse react when the old man split the rock?
3 How does the writer use contrast to make the meeting with the strange old man more exciting?

C The story takes place in various settings. Copy and complete this table, making notes on each different setting and the part of the plot that takes place there.

Setting	Plot
Alderley hill – October, dawn	Farmer riding from Mobberley, on his way to Macclesfield fair

Vocabulary

Word games

As well as being fun, **word games** can help you to learn tricky spellings and to increase your vocabulary.

A This crossword puzzle, based on 'The Legend of Alderley', has been filled in with all the answers, but the clues are missing. Write a clue to go with each answer.

CLUES	
Down	Acros
1	2
3	4
5	6
7	9
8	

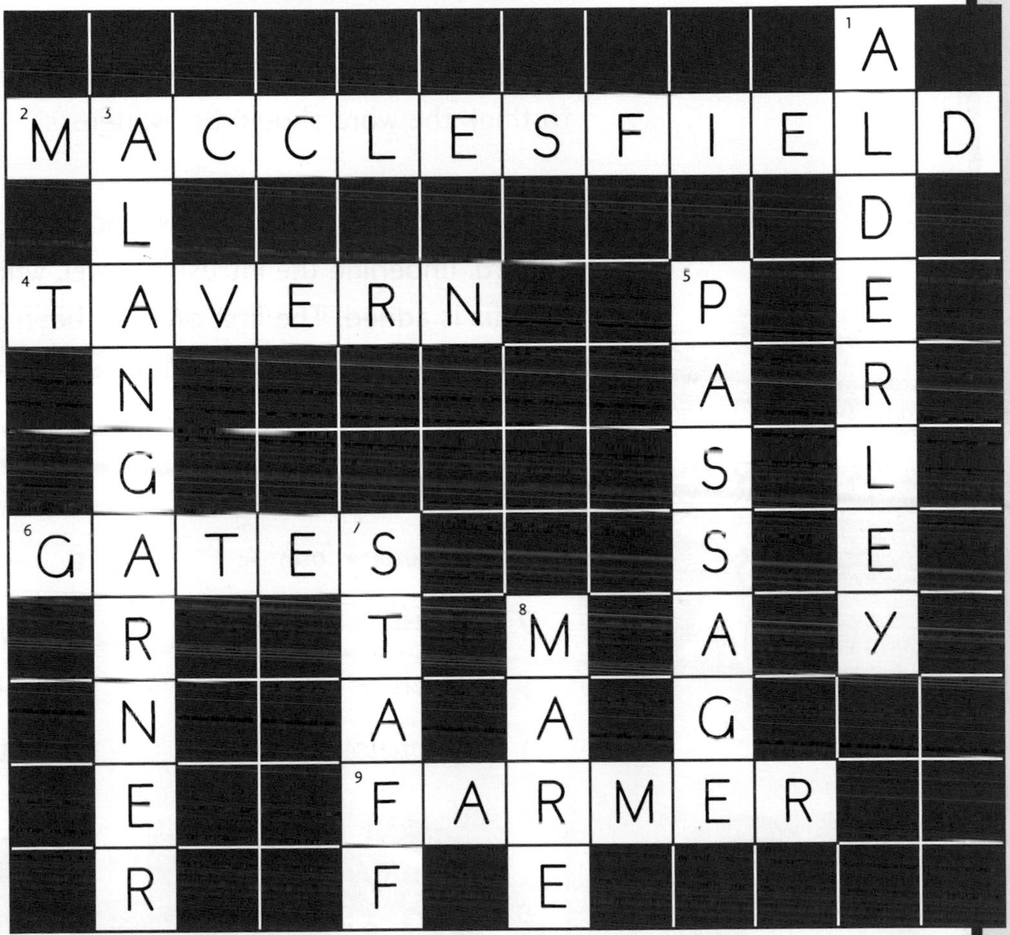

1 A L D E R L E Y
2 M A C C L E S F I E L D
3 A L T A N G A R N E R
4 T A V E R N
5 P A S S A G E
6 G A T E S
7 S T A F F
8 M A R E
9 F A R M E R

B Make up a crossword of your own. It is a good idea to draw a grid of squares first, then to think of some clues and use a pencil to work out where the answers could go on the grid. Then, write the number of each clue next to the right square on the grid, fill the blank squares in black and rub out your pencilled answers. Challenge a friend to answer the questions and complete the crossword.

Spelling

Intrusive vowels

Remember, **unstressed vowels** are vowels which we either do not sound, or do not sound very distinctly, as we speak. Unlike unstressed vowels, **intrusive vowels** are letters we think might be in a word when they are not!

Intrusive vowels often occur in words to which a suffix has been added, which has resulted in a letter being dropped. It is tempting to think that the letter is still there. For example, the feminine of 'waiter' is 'waitress'. In adding the suffix 'ess' to 'waiter', we drop the 'e', but it would be easy to think the word should be 'wait<u>e</u>ress'.

A Copy each 'word sum' below and write the answer. In the original word, underline the intrusive vowel, which is dropped when the suffix is added. The first one has been done to help you. Use a dictionary to check your answers.

1. winter + 'y' = wintry
2. generous + 'ity' =
3. disaster + 'ous' =
4. exclaim + 'ation' =
5. humour + 'ous' =
6. curious + 'ity' =
7. monster + 'ous' =
8. tiger + 'ess' =
9. carpenter + 'y' =
10. enter + 'ance' =
11. pronounce + 'ation' =
12. emperor + 'ess' =

B Choose six of the trickier words from part A and write a mnemonic for each one, to help you remember how to spell it.

Grammar

Personal and impersonal writing

In **personal writing**, the writer uses personal pronouns.
For example:

 <u>I</u> thought *The Weirdstone of Brisingamen* was excellent, and think <u>you</u> would like it, too.

In **impersonal writing**, the writer avoids using personal pronouns, uses the impersonal pronoun 'it' and makes generalised statements.
For example:

 The Weirdstone of Brisingamen is an excellent book, which many people would enjoy.

Changing sentences from personal to impersonal, or the other way round, can slightly alter the meaning.

A Rewrite these sentences, changing them from personal to impersonal.

1 My friends and I think the legend is unlikely to be true.

2 Our reason for thinking this is that we can't believe the cave wouldn't have been discovered by somebody else.

3 Whatever the truth, I found the book a great read!

B Change these sentences from impersonal to personal.

1 Children often find it difficult to know when to use semi-colons.

2 It is said to be straightforward if the guidelines are followed.

3 The appropriate use of punctuation considerably improves the quality of writing.

Punctuation

Using semi-colons

Remember, **semi-colons** are used instead of a conjunction to join the clauses in a compound sentence. In 'The Legend of Alderley', Alan Garner sometimes uses semi-colons, rather than conjunctions or shorter sentences, to make his writing flow well. For example:

The horse should stay; he did not want her.

A Copy a sentence from the passage in which the author has used semi-colons. Write it again, using shorter sentences, with full stops in place of the semi-colons. Which version do you think is better? Give your reasons.

B Rewrite the following sentences, changing them to include semi-colons rather than conjunctions.

1 The farmer was totally perplexed because nobody at the fair offered to buy his mare.

2 The farmer was terrified, so he offered to give the mare to the wizard.

3 The farmer was dazzled by the treasure and he grabbed as much as he could carry.

Writing

Extended stories

Extended stories – long stories – do not necessarily have more characters than very short stories. However, they usually have a variety of settings, and a plot that is made up of several events rather than just one or two. At the beginning of 'The Legend of Alderley', the main character – the farmer – is on Alderley Hill,

then moves on to Thieves' Hole,

and then to the town of Macclesfield,

before returning to Thieves' Hole.

From there, he and the wizard travel to the great rock

and into a cave, where they enter two chambers.

Finally, the farmer finds himself outside the rock, on a hill near Stormy Point. The action of the story takes place over a day, beginning at dawn and ending at night.

You are going to plan and write an extended story of your own, called 'A Strange Encounter'.

1 Plan your story:
   - Make a rough plan of the plot so you know all the things that are going to happen in your story and the order in which they happen.
   - Decide on the number, names and personalities of the characters. Just because this is going to be an 'extended' story does not mean you have to have a large number of characters. Often the most successful stories have only two or three characters.
   - Think carefully about the various settings you need, so you can move the plot of the story to different places. Have at least three different settings.

2 Write your first draft. Make sure you describe the characters and settings in detail so that the reader has a clear picture of them. Then, proofread and revise your draft, and present your final copy, giving it an interesting title.

Cat Tales

The Cheshire Cat

This is an extract from *Alice's Adventures in Wonderland* by Lewis Carroll, in which Alice meets the Cheshire Cat. It is just one of many strange adventures!

The Cat only grinned when it saw Alice. It looked good-natured, she thought; still it had *very* long claws and a great many teeth, so she felt that it ought to be treated with respect.

"Cheshire Puss," she began, rather timidly, as she did not at all know whether it would like the name. However, it only grinned a little wider. "Come, it's pleased so far," thought Alice, and she went on. "Would you like to tell me, please, which way I ought to go from here?"

"That depends a good deal on where you want to get to," said the Cat.

"I don't much care where –" said Alice.

"Then it doesn't matter which way you go," said the Cat.

"– so long as I get *somewhere*," Alice added as an explanation.

"Oh, you're sure to do that," said the Cat, "if you only walk long enough."

Alice felt that this could not be denied, so she tried another question. "What sort of people live about here?"

"In *that* direction," the Cat said, waving its right paw around, "lives a Hatter, and in *that* direction," waving the other paw, "lives a March Hare. Visit either you like; they're both mad."

"But I don't want to go among mad people," Alice remarked.

"Oh, you can't help that," said the Cat, "we're all mad here. I'm mad. You're mad."

"How do you know I'm mad?" said Alice.

"You must be," said the Cat, "or you wouldn't have come here."

Alice didn't think that proved it at all; however, she went on,

"And how do you know that you're mad?"

"To begin with," said the Cat, "a dog's not mad. You grant that?"

"I suppose so," said Alice.

"Well, then," the Cat went on, "you see a dog growls when it's angry, and wags its tail when it's pleased. Now *I* growl when I'm pleased, and wag my tail when I'm angry. Therefore I'm mad."

"*I* call it purring, not growling," said Alice.

"Call it what you like," said the Cat. "Do you play croquet with the Queen today?"

"I should like it very much," said Alice, "but I haven't been invited yet."

"You'll see me there," said the Cat, and vanished.

Cat and the Weather

Cat takes a look at the weather,
Snow.
Puts a paw on the sill.
His perch is piled, is a pillow.

Shape of pad appears.
Will it dig? No.
Not like sand
Like his fur almost.

But licked, not liked.
Too cold.
Insects are flying, fainting down.
He'll try

to bat one against the pane.
They have no body and no buzz.
And now his feet are wet;
it's a puzzle.

Shakes each leg,
then shakes his skin
to get the white flies off.
Looks for his tail

tells it to come on in
by the radiator.
World's turned queer
somehow. All white,

no smell. Well, here
inside it's still familiar.
He'll go to sleep until
it puts itself to right.

by May Swenson

Comprehension

Although they are by different writers, the two pieces of writing share the theme of cats. Each, however, explores a different aspect of cats, and in a different way. Look again at the passage from *Alice's Adventures in Wonderland*, and answer the questions below. Then look again at 'Cat and the Weather' and answer the same questions.

1   What type of writing is it?
2   For what purpose do you think it was written?
3   For what audience do you think it was written?
4   Does it rely on what the writer has seen or on his/her imagination?
5   In what kind of book would you find it?

 **Vocabulary**

Puns

> A **pun** is a humorous play on words. Puns are often based on having two possible meanings. Many puns involve homophones or homonyms.
> For example:
>> Leila had a toothache. Brian said, "Put your head through the window and the <u>pain</u> will be gone."

A Can you explain these puns?
   1   Headline on a sports page: 'Marathon Runner's Great Feat'.
   2   "I hope this dragon story doesn't drag on too long," said Ian.
   3   "You can't beat eggs," said the chef.
   4   Second-hand coat for sale – only slightly worn.
   5   "Your fiancée is very late for the wedding," said the vicar. "I'll give her a ring," replied the groom.
   6   Question: What do you call a man with a seagull on his head.
       Answer: Cliff

B Make up a few puns of your own. Make a list of some homophones and homonyms and try putting them into sentences so that the sentence has a double meaning.

Spelling

Words within words

Remember, it makes spelling easier if you can find smaller words within a longer word, and can help you to remember more difficult words. For example 'disinterested' contains the words: I, is, sin, in, interested, interest, rested, rest, inter.

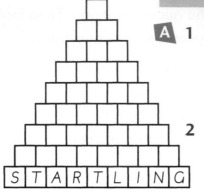

A 1 The word 'startling' can be changed into eight other common words by removing one letter at a time from different places in the word. Copy and complete the word pyramid opposite. You are not allowed to use a letter once you have taken it out!

2 Find and write down all the words you can find hidden in 'therein'. You should be able to find at least eight! You don't have to rearrange the letters.

| S | T | A | R | T | L | I | N | G |

B Use a dictionary to help you identify the words below. All the words begin with 'cat'. The first one has been done to help you.

1 used for hurling small stones *catapult*
2 small furry flower of a tree
3 fashion models walk along this
4 a type of fish
5 a very large church
6 list of things for sale
7 to grab a moving object, like a ball
8 the larva of a butterfly or moth
9 the Pope's religion
10 a short sleep
11 large farm animals
12 a disaster

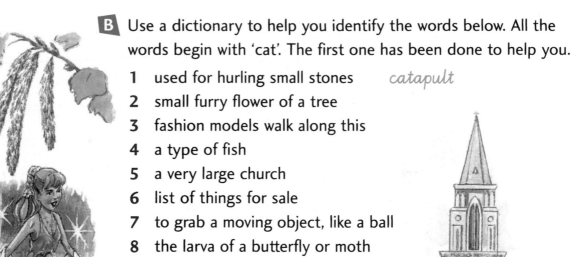

Grammar

Word classes

Remember, there are eight **word classes**, or parts of speech: **nouns**, **pronouns**, **adjectives**, **verbs**, **adverbs**, **prepositions**, **conjunctions** and **interjections**. The four most important are: nouns, adjectives, verbs and adverbs.

Many words can be altered by adding or taking away various prefixes and suffixes. Some words can have several forms, so that they can become each of these four word classes.

A Copy and complete the table below. Use your dictionary to check your spelling, and use the 'word tester' before you add each word to the table.

> **Word tester**
> Nouns: I noticed his/her/its _____ .
> Adjectives: This is very _____ .
> Verbs: He/she may _____ this.
> Adverbs: It was done _____ .

Noun	Adjective	Verb	Adverb
respect	respectful	respect	respectably
			amazingly
		agree	
			satisfactorily
	pitiful		
playfulness			
		boast	
	irritable		
reliability			

B Write a silly sentence which includes all the following words:

enjoy   enjoyable   enjoyment   enjoyably

Sentence construction

Passive sentences

Remember, some **passive sentences** do not always state who or what is doing the action of the verb. For example:

The <u>cat</u> was <u>chased</u> along the road.

subject   passive verb

We do not know who or what was chasing the cat. The sentence could have read:

The cat was chased along the road <u>by a dog</u>.

A Rewrite these passive sentences so that they do not reveal who or what did the action.

1 Alice was suddenly startled by the Cat.

2 The Cheshire Cat was amused by Alice.

3 The Cat was asked a number of questions by Alice.

4 Alice was given some strange and confusing answers by the Cat.

5 She was surprised by the Cat's sudden disappearance.

B Rewrite the sentences in part A, turning them into active sentences. The first one has been done to help you.

1 The cat suddenly startled Alice.

Writing

Writing styles

You are going to write about cats in two very different **styles**. The way you write needs to be different each time, because each piece has a different purpose. One piece of writing is going to be narrative (a story), and the other is going to be descriptive (a description, without a story).

1 Narrative writing

Choose whether your story about cats will be:

- a ghost story
- a mystery story
- a science-fiction story
- a picture story for young children, with pictures and text.

For narrative writing, you need to:

- plan the plot
- plan the characters
- plan the setting
- decide whether to include dialogue
- plan the beginning and the ending
- write your first draft
- proofread and revise your first draft
- present your final copy.

2 Descriptive writing

Choose whether to write:

- a piece of poetry
- a piece of prose (non-rhyming text).

Decide whether to describe a cat:

- asleep
- at play.

For descriptive writing, you need to consider:

- using adjectives
- using adverbs
- describing details
- writing your first draft
- proofreading and revising your first draft
- writing your final copy.

Check-up

 Vocabulary

A Write a homophone to match each of these words.

1 hole   2 board   3 feat   4 road

5 groan   6 site   7 tale   8 wood

B The underlined words in the sentences below are homonyms. Use each word in a sentence of your own, so that it has a different meaning.

1 My library book was overdue so I had to pay a <u>fine</u>.

2 The <u>bear</u> gave a roar.

3 The traffic <u>jam</u> was huge.

4 I saw her <u>trip</u> over the boxes.

C Write the modern version of each word below.

1 shalt   2 yonder   3 wilt

4 spake   5 gavest   6 thou

D 1 Which month is named after:

    a Mars, the Roman god of war?   b the Latin word for 'eight'?

    c Julius Caesar?   d the Roman word for 'ten'?

2 Which day of the week is named after:

    a the Moon?   b the goddess Freya?

    c the planet Saturn?   d the god Thor?

E Write six words that people living 100 years ago wouldn't have known.

F Give two definitions for each word – firstly, its original meaning, and then its more modern one.

1 crash   2 mobile   3 wild   4 file

G Copy and complete these idioms.

1 to be _____ with envy

2 to be a snake in the _____

3 to take a shot in the _____

4 a drop in the _____

5 set the ball _____

6 out of the frying pan, into the _____

H Think of an anagram for each of the following words. The anagram can have more than one word.

1 teacher   2 homework   3 elephant   4 football

Spelling

A Copy each pair of words, underline the common 'root' and use a dictionary to find the meaning of each root and its origin.

1 auditorium   audience

2 aquarium   aquatic

3 hydrant   hydraulic

4 memory   memorundum

B For each word below, write three more words from the same word family.

1 achieve   2 respect   3 complete   4 concern

C Copy each word and divide it into its syllables.

1 separate   2 confusion   3 difficulty   4 punch

D Make up mnemonics to help you remember how to spell two of these words.

difficult   stationary   secretary   parliament   separate

E 1 Copy each word and circle the unstressed letter.

a secretary   b usually   c castle   d offering

e rustle   f often   g conscious   h general

2 Write the correct spelling of each word, adding the unstressed letter.

a hasen   b jewllery   c brisle   d voluntry

e seprate   f duspan   g choclate   h exitement

F 1 Write the correct spelling of each of the following words.

    a *actoress*   b *labourious*   c *reclaimation*   d *monsterous*

  2 What do all the words have in common?

G Write down all the words you can find 'hidden' within each of the following words.

  1 *unimportant*   2 *inconsiderate*   3 *rediscover*   4 *uncontrollable*

Grammar

A Copy the underlined words in each sentence. Next to each word, state what word class it is in the sentence.

  1 The <u>large</u> <u>black</u> <u>dog</u> <u>ran</u> <u>swiftly</u> <u>through</u> the <u>long</u> <u>wet</u> <u>grass</u>.

  2 <u>Hey!</u> <u>Put</u> down that <u>valuable</u> <u>vase</u> <u>immediately</u>.

B Copy and complete these sentences by adding a subject and an object. Underline the subject and circle the object.

  1 _____ *jumped over* _____.

  2 _____ *fell into* _____.

  3 _____ *swam towards* _____.

C Make a compound sentence from each of these pairs of sentences. Draw a circle around each conjunctions.

  1 *My sister had a baby last week. She has called her Alice.*

  2 *I bought the baby a red dress. It is my sister's favourite colour.*

D Copy the verb in each sentence. State whether it is active or passive.

  1 *My dog eats shoes.*

  2 *Our cat stole the fish from the table.*

  3 *The seed was eaten by the birds.*

E Write each sentence correctly.

1 I seen a big fish in the pond.

2 We is going out tonight.

3 She have done the painting.

4 He has came with me on holiday.

5 I done most of the sums.

6 You was really rude to her.

7 They was really late again.

8 I were only trying to help.

F Write whether each sentence is an example of personal or impersonal writing.

1 I always visit my Gran on a Tuesday night.

2 The elderly people enjoyed a game of cards.

3 We won the match, but it was very close.

4 Football is a very popular sport all over the world.

G Write two examples of each of the following types of word class.

1 noun

2 verb

3 adjective

4 adverb

5 preposition

6 conjunction

Punctuation and sentence construction

A Copy this paragraph, adding the missing punctuation and capital letters.

my closest friends are charlotte lydia sophie and emma we usually eat our lunch together and try to sit together in class emma whose sister is in my brothers class says shes really going to miss us when her family moves to nottingham in july

B Use each of these connectives in a sentence of your own.

1 whilst on the other hand

2 but none the less

C Write two sentences, one that contains a colon and one that contains a semi-colon.

D 1 Expand this sentence, using an adjective phrase or clause.

On the wall hung a painting.

2 Expand this sentence, using an adverb phrase or clause.

Everyone began eating.

E Using not more than 100 words, write a summary of a story you have read.

F 1 Rewrite the following passive sentences, so that they state who or what did the action of the verb.

　　a *The tree was cut down.*

　　b *The washing was hung on the line.*

　　c *The path was swept.*

　　2 Rewrite your answers to question 1, changing them from passive to active.

Writing

Choose one of the following ways of writing about the starting point.

> STARTING POINT: A strange happening
>
> You are going to write about something that people will find it hard to believe. Whatever you write, you need to think carefully about:
>
> - what happened (plot)
> - who is involved (characters)
> - where it happened (setting)
> - whether you will write in the first person or the third person(unless you are writing a playscript or a poem).

> Write a mystery story involving a strange happening. Is the mystery solved or will it remain a puzzle forever?

> Write a poem about a strange happening. How do you want your readers to feel when they read the poem – scared, sad, happy, puzzled, amazed?

> Write about a strange happening in the form of a playscript.

> Imagine the strange happening was a ghostly encounter. Write a ghost story which will keep the readers on the edge of their seats.

> Write a science-fiction story about a strange happening. Does it take place here on Earth or on another planet?